FIGHTING DEATH

And Other
Desperate Battles

By Peter D. Wyns

D1280302

Great Reward Publishing

Great Reward Publishing
PO Box 36324
Rock Hill, SC 29732
803-324-0739
www.peterwyns.org
e-mail: wynsusa@comporium.net

Second Printing, January 2007

First Great Reward Publishing edition published 2005

ISBN 10: 0-9771633-0-X
ISBN 13: 978-0-9771633-0-4

Manufactured in the United States of America
by BooksJustBooks

Contents

I dedicate this book to my wife, Joy

Like other wives worthy of nobility, she stands as a life anchor behind her husband and children. She serves tirelessly with domestic responsibilities, often receiving insufficient praise for all she does. This has never hindered her from being a spiritual woman. She is always the first to believe, the first to love, and the first to pray. When trouble comes, she moves from the domestic scene to the front lines. She has fought for her family with more vigilance than a dozen soldiers. Like iron set in concrete, she has faced the wind, held the family together, and made the difference. Thank you, Joy, for fighting for our children and for standing with me through every storm. Thank you for being a woman of outstanding faith.

Breaking Through

The crowd was unwieldy as it edged its way along the dusty, village road. No one was spared from the push and shove of the mob; the strongest men held the most privileged positions close to the epicenter. Tough women would not be denied, and street-smart children who had learned to be rough pressed in and held their ground as well. The noise was so loud that it was difficult to hear a neighbor speak. The hustle grew more intense as the mob increased in size. If panic had a chance to spark, violence was only a step away. No one had taken charge of this mob, and the hundreds of delegates were now becoming thousands. It was not a political rally or a violent protest, although an uninformed observer might have thought so. No, it was the miracle worker. He had come to town. Both skeptics and believers crowded in to see and perhaps touch him. They did not know when he would perform his next wonder, but when he did, they would be there to witness it.

She was bent over, hidden in her clothes, as if ashamed of her appearance. She had been sick for twelve years, and no physician had conjured a potion or mixed a medicine to stop her blood letting. She had spent her last bit of money looking for solutions, but there were none. For days at a time she was so weak and physically helpless that she could not work or even get around. She was unable to accomplish the most menial tasks. Her survival was due to the kindness of others. They brought her scraps of food or, from time to time, placed a coin in her hand. Hope for healing had died many years ago. She had all but resigned herself to her humiliating condition.

Amazing as it sounds, through all of her sorrows, she had not turned bitter or criminal. She had a faith in God and lived in the place of secret prayer. Her spirit found a measure of solace and peace in that secret place. True, she had lost hope for physical change, but not for her soul or for eternal life at the end of the journey. She even had moments of great pleasure, because she found satisfaction through helping someone less fortunate than herself. In small but meaningful ways, she assisted many. She looked for opportunities to feed and clothe the worst of the village beggars. It was her faith and generosity of heart that caused the townspeople to give more alms to her than to those beggars who wore bitter dispositions. She was no beggar, just destitute. People were moved to compassion and generosity.

She saw him from a distance. Days before, she had listened to his voice as he taught the multitude and performed miracles. He spoke of the living God. She knew he was no fake. He was a holy man. He slipped away that day before she could reach him. Now the word was out—he was coming into the city. The skeptics in the crowd did not concern her. This day, whatever the cost to body or soul, she would touch the man of God. If she were stronger, she would have traveled into the countryside to find him. The crowds would have been much lighter, but that was not feasible. No, her plan was to pray and ask God to help her get through the mob. Many others in need of healing and help would be trying to do the same. Normally she would be glad to step back and let another go first, but not today. This was her day. She was desperate, and no one could deny her.

She heard the noise of the mob before it appeared. Slowly she made her way to the center of the road. The crowd moved as one entity. It came toward her like an ocean, not fast but forceful. When the multitude hit, she struggled to remain on her feet like one wading into the surf as it crashes upon the beach. She was jostled and bumped by unstoppable waves of people, but she refused to fall. She held on to whomever she could, using their bodies like a chain to pull herself deeper into the middle of the throng. It did not matter what they thought. She had to reach the rabbi at any cost.

She could see him now but not consistently. He was not tall, and she was bent over, so she often lost him in the crowd. She stretched earnestly and caught sight of him again. He was getting closer. Soon he would walk past, but she was cutting the angle toward him. Others were holding their place in the mob, moving with it in forward motion. She was like a salmon swimming upstream. She knew her target and was bound and determined to reach him. Yelling to him was useless, because he would never hear her. Even if he did, what would her voice mean among so many? She pressed forward, gaining ground, not because she was strong in body, but because she was strong in spirit.

Suddenly, an elbow rose up and struck her in the face. She felt dizzy and dazed and almost blacked out. Her eyes watered and it became difficult for her to see. Pain shot through her feeble frame. This would leave a nasty bruise, but she gathered composure and pushed forward. Her legs were wobbly from exertion and told her she should give up. She dug in even harder, ignoring the trauma of the moment because she would not be deterred from her quest. She pushed and weaved her way with an energy that surprised her. She broke through the crowd and came upon the man of God just as he passed by. With a final thrust she turned sideways, squeezed her body forward through a tight gap of bodies and fell. Her arm was fully extended and she stretched with all of her might. Before hitting the ground, she grasped the hem of the rabbi's robe and yanked it back. Immediately, she felt virtue flush through her body like a bucket of cold spring water that had suddenly been poured over her hot and dusty frame. She knew instantly that she was healed of her disease. The presence of the Almighty filled her entire being as a supernatural heat moved up her arm and touched her heart.

She would have been trampled, but suddenly the crowd came to a halt. Jesus had stopped and turned. The clumsy mob fell in upon itself. He stopped, and they stopped, and everyone watched intently to see what he was about to do. "Who touched me?" he said loudly. "Who touched my clothes?" (Luke 8:45)

A hush rippled through the multitude. For a moment a nervous, almost awkward stillness hung in the air. People tried to step back and make room. They were puzzled. Peter said, "Master, the people are crowding and pressing against you." (Luke 8:45 NIV)

But Jesus said, "Someone touched me; I know that power has gone out from me." (Luke 8:46 NIV)

Finally the woman made herself known, and Jesus said, "Daughter, your faith has healed you. Go in peace." (Luke 8:48 NIV)

This woman was determined to reach God. With only a gift of faith, she had broken through the crowd, fought the battle, and won the presence and power of God. She set in motion the plan for her healing. Jesus was amazed when it happened. He commended her for her faith, and heaven yielded its supernatural power. She was healed.

Clarice Holden is a modern-day equivalent of this fighting woman. Her husband's accident would leave him on the threshold of death. If it had been other people, at another time, in another place, he would have died, but not here and not today.

From an impossible situation Clarice rose up, fought the fight, and took hold of the hem of Christ's robe. She would not be denied. God's healing power brought miracle after miracle. Everyone was surprised—even the death angel seemed taken aback. From the doorway of death, Ronnie Holden returned to the land of the living, and he returned with grace and gifts that come only from God.

This is the story of Ronnie and Clarice Holden. As strange as it may seem, it is absolutely true in every detail. May it inspire you and help you to fight the battles you face. It is time to rise up, by God's grace, and overcome the impossible hardships. May you be blessed like those throughout the ages who have prayed desperate prayers, fought desperate battles, and reached the heart of God. I pray, by God's grace, that you also may receive a miracle. "For nothing is impossible with God." (Luke 1:37 NIV)

—Peter Wyns

Part One

Fighting for Life

Chapter 1

The Healing Wave

Hiding his pain, Ronnie Holden looked down at the Shallotte River as he forced his leg to step into position and leave the mainland. He was boarding Island Breeze, the fifty-three-foot, Grand Banks trawler yacht that would become his winter vacation home for the next month or so. He and his wife, Clarice, were setting sail from the shores of Shallotte, North Carolina, bound for the Florida Keys. The naysayers had told them they should not go. After all, it was impossible that Robbie was even alive. Who would believe such an outlandish story, and who could navigate the emotional heights of this past year? Clarice could still hear the words screaming in her head, "Just tonight, let him live. Let's just get through this awful night. Nothing else matters."

She unloaded the bag of perishables into the galley fridge and turned to watch Ronnie find his seat and catch his breath. She smiled at her partner. They were inseparable, and not just because they had shared thirty-one years of marriage. No, it was much more than that. They had faced death together, and after the ancient enemy exhaled his cloud of foul breath over them, they rose up, wrestled him to the ground, and won. Death was on them and all around them, and at times no glint of light was able to pass through the ominous shadow of his dark robe. They fought, and others came and fought with them. With frail, human strokes, they swung the sword of undeserved faith against an enemy far greater than they. It was a David-against-Goliath-type battle, and the Lord attended them. He stood by their side through the midnight storm until their feeble sword penetrated the impenetrable shroud, and life poked through where life was not supposed to be.

Clarice smiled with a thought of relief and unspoken thankfulness as the wind caught the lip of Ronnie's sun-bleached hair and lifted it off his brow. He had said, "I want everyone to know what God has done. I will not shrink back or faint away from that which we have always done. We will continue with the plan of life, the same—yet at the same time, never the same again."

I wonder whether there has ever been a more stubborn yet godly couple than this? Randy, the captain's mate, was on board to help, but Ronnie was determined to pilot his own ship, as he always did. The engines soon roared, and the marshy backwaters of the river gave way to the Intracoastal Waterway. They continued on course for several days until the ship found its way out past the port of Miami and into the wide Atlantic.

It was early December, Ronnie's famous Twin Lakes restaurant was closed for the season, and Clarice's Island Breeze clothing store had been placed in good hands. Good hands indeed, but not like the hands that held this noble crew in place. Folks knew that the very hands of God were cupped around this boat. Calling it "The Holy Boat" or "Heaven's Boat" would not have seemed inappropriate, for if God were not with the Holdens, then he was with none of humankind. Indeed, he was with them. His shadow was cast over them, and they were upheld in his mighty arms. Their very lives were testimony to the great love and care that he extends to his children.

Soon they turned the ship from south to southwest and laid eyes on the beautiful Florida Keys, a string of islands like a pearl necklace that stretches 100 miles into the Gulf of Mexico. This archipelago is so different from the rest of mainland America that a man who allowed his thoughts to drift might assume that he had reached some distant, tropical paradise.

Almost a century before, bridges were engineered, and a railroad linked the islands, right out to their extreme, knife-like tip: Key West. A significant shipping port was established here, providing a new trade route to Central and South America. It was successful for a time, but it did not last. A hurricane tore it to pieces in 1935, and it was never replaced. Instead, U.S. Highway 1 was extended in 1938 to connect the islands. Better bridges were built, including one measuring seven miles long. They supported roads, not rails, opening the Keys to anyone with a roadworthy vehicle and a spirit of adventure. Just south of the Florida Everglades, the now-accessible vacation spot lured thousands of sun seekers to turquoise shallows and warm, sandy beaches.

The Holdens were well-accustomed to life on the seas, but this journey was like no other. As the constant waves lapped the sides of the boat and the pelicans spread glider wings to fly in perfect, almost sacred formation, the Spirit of God came with holy waves of warm refreshment. He sent those waves deep into the dry and weary crevices of their souls as medicine the likes of which are not found in any hospital. It seemed that old doors in the basements of their hearts, like forgotten, dungeon doors in an ancient castle, were slowly being pried open for light and life to flood them once again. Until now, they had not fully realized how tired and utterly exhausted they were from the intensity of the battle they had fought. The fight had exacted years from their lives like those whose lives are cut short from heavy labor or severe trauma, but now, hour by soothing hour, God was giving those years back to them. They were being rebuilt with godly wonder, inspiration, and quiet recreation.

Time went to sleep and worry fell away as fish leapt from the water, and birds skipped across the crests of the waves. Dolphins played alongside the boat, and billowy clouds looked down from above to study the Holdens' healing process. All creation sang around them, for the triumph of God's grace was now the cloak that caressed them. It was no longer the grim garment of death, but life that sheltered and shadowed them. Here, on the open sea, God's healing mantle stretched to the distant horizon.

The sun was lowering, and the sky was intensified with hues of cadmium and crimson. Yellows turned to orange and purple reds until the entire expanse of the western heavens were ablaze with the glory of God's paintbrush. It was just too much for Ronnie. His eyes grew moist, and the dams of Holden emotions burst open as the finger of God pushed gently into the depths of his soul. "It is so beautiful, so magnificent," Ronnie whispered, as tears fell from his eyes and began rolling, one after the other, down his cheeks. "If I had died, if you had not prayed, if God had not come," he could hardly contain his thoughts, "I would not have seen this sunset. I would not be here. I would be gone. I would have missed it."

He held Clarice in a firm embrace as he continued to weep unashamedly and wipe the tears now dripping off his chin. She held him warmly with a bursting heart so full of emotion that she could not speak. There they remained for the longest time, and, in the Spirit, the same master who washed his other disciples' feet many centuries before washed their feet. What a delightfully, stubborn couple they had been; what a wonderful world it was; what an awesome God they had.

Chapter 2

God's Way or No Way

C larice did not come from a churchgoing family, but her mother's best friend, Ms. Vertilee Bennett, would pick her up every week and take her to Sunday school. There she made an early confession of salvation, but as many children do, she soon wandered from those formative, foundations of faith. Clarice always felt loved by her dad, even though his life was less than ideal. When she was 17, her father had cancer surgery, and this frightened him sufficiently that he surrendered his life to Christ. He stopped drinking and began attending church. Her mother refused to go even though, by all accounts, she was a good woman. She worked extremely hard, and some would say she was driven. Perhaps this was her way of escaping reality. Perhaps it was her subconscious attempt at maintaining dignity and producing something worthwhile in life.

Ronnie's Christian heritage went back for at least a few generations. His Grandpa Holden was an ardent churchgoer and Christian leader. He was one of a team of men that was responsible for the building of more than one church in the community. Ronnie's mom was a believer, but his dad was a quiet man who kept to himself and made no claims of religion or the Christian faith. Ronnie's mother took him to a Baptist Sunday school and prayed for his to be a life lived for God. Like Clarice, it was there in Sunday school that he made an early confession of Jesus as savior.

Pleasure and self-absorption have often been the distractions that conspire to channel the attention of many teens away from God. It happened to Ronnie, and his passion for fun and adventure soon became the focus of his life. Consequently he fell prey to a self-destructive life directed by selfish gratification.

When he married Clarice in 1969, he thought he was in full control of life. He had the woman he wanted, started a restaurant six months after marriage to acquire wealth, and was focused on his quest for adventure. He lived life to the max, swallowing as much pleasure as he could along the way. The more he fed his passions, however, the more his life turned sour. This path led to the road of shallow and empty pursuits, and eventually Ronnie began experimenting with alcohol and drugs. It takes time for a confident, self-made man to lose his way, but Ronnie had no anchor to hold him in the storm. He became hopelessly addicted to cocaine.

As the years passed, Clarice realized that she was married to a changing person, and the changes were not good. Ronnie had become irritable, impatient, and irresponsible. His frustrations made him obnoxious, and more often than not he was angry with life and with everyone around him. It was no longer fun being married to this man.

Often he was away from home for days at a time, without giving any notice of his whereabouts or mentioning when he would return. Clarice fought hard to hold her marriage together, but she had her own problems. She was suffering with chronic sickness. She fainted three or four times a day, and her body was under constant attack from one disease or another. Once she fainted while sitting behind the wheel of her car. She was waiting in line for the bridge to open. Finally the driver in the car behind her came to her window after the bridge opened and she did not move.

Her internal organs began to fail, and Clarice was in and out of the hospital for surgeries and treatments. On one occasion her hospital stay extended seventy-five days, as medical professionals tried to discover the cause of her prolific fainting spells. The doctors were unable to solve her problem. They could only say that her dilemma was stress-related, and they had no choice but to send her home.

She argued and fought with Ronnie and attempted to put him straight, but this only worsened their failing relationship. Chaos and confusion surrounded them, and their lives became a story of grief and pain. Everything went downhill, and even the business slipped into disrepair. If not for Clarice and her hard work at the restaurant, they would have lost it and been forced into bankruptcy.

Regardless of the personal scenarios or traumas we are caught in, life continues around us, and in 1981, tragedy struck. Ms. Vertilee's husband, Captain Harry, had a heart attack. He and Ms. Vertilee were out on the Calabash River on their boat. It was the first day of shrimp season, and Captain Harry had a massive coronary. He died before reaching the shore. Clarice loved this elderly couple. They were like second parents to her, and the loss of Captain Harry hit hard.

Clarice was struggling with sorrow and grief as she entered Ms. Vertilee's home for the funeral wake a couple of days later. What she saw was not at all what she expected. People were happy; they were laughing and enjoying themselves. "He was a fine Christian," they said. "He's gone to heaven. He's with Jesus now."

Clarice believed it to be true—there must be life after death—but this behavior did not seem quite right. She had never seen anything like this before and was trying to grasp and understand the inappropriate activity in the room when Nell Eaddy, the pastor's wife, approached her and said, "Do you know the Lord?"

She was scared to death and felt so empty. Clarice was far from God. She was desperate, and with honest humility she answered, "No, I do not know the Lord." At that moment she reached out for that which could not be possible. She reached for hope beyond hope. She reached and took hold of God. As if the event were especially designed for her, folks gathered around her in holy agreement as she repented of her sins and said the sinner's prayer. Clarice yielded her life to Christ and became a born-again Christian at Captain Harry's funeral. What an experience! Joy and lightness brought relief to the worn-out fiber of her frail soul, and a brilliant new tapestry for living began weaving its way into her life. The weight of unbearable burdens lifted, as depression and despair were replaced by hope and inexplicable excitement.

When Clarice shared her new beginning, Ronnie wouldn't hear it. He said, "Those people are crazy, and I don't want you to have anything to do with them. People who go to church are weak people. They have just found a crutch to lean on, but it is not reality, and I want you to stay away." Clarice could not stay away, and instead of improving, their marriage worsened. Sunday after Sunday Ronnie would say, "If you're going to church, I'm going out to get drunk," and he usually did.

The church began praying for him, but his salvation was nowhere in sight. Church members came to the home to encourage Clarice and befriend Ronnie. In response, Ronnie openly insulted them and did his best to be rude and find a way to drive them off. Their marriage became a living hell for Clarice, and her only escape was to live in her newly found heaven—the fellowship of the local church. Ronnie's cocaine habit began to control his entire existence. He took sleeping pills, Valium, and other drugs to try to keep him at home, but every night he was driven to leave the house. He had become a slave, chained to a drug and led by a force more powerful than he. Ronnie was helpless. He could not resist his new master.

One night he got into his car and three days later found himself eight hundred miles away in Miami. He remembered nothing from the moment he left home and did not know how he got to Miami. One morning, just as the sun was rising, Ronnie dragged his tortured and tormented body into the house. He had been gone for several days without so much as a word to Clarice, and there she was now, standing in front of him. Clarice spoke up, "Can I make you some breakfast, Ronnie?"

This was all Ronnie could stand. He understood her anger, arguments, and retaliation against him. He deserved that, but her kindness he could not abide. He did not know how to handle undeserved grace, and he exploded. "Are you crazy? Have you lost your mind? You need to see a psychiatrist or something. You're just not right, woman."

Ronnie's mind would not shift because of ardent arguments or coercive criticism, but his heart was finally moved by tenderness and compassion, and his guard fell. "I need help," he whispered. That opened the door and led the way for Ronnie to be admitted at Fenwick Hall Rehabilitation Center on John's Island, South Carolina.

The rehab center was not a faith-based organization, and, as far as the Holdens knew, no Christians were there during the time of Ronnie's stay. It cost $12,000 a month for detoxification treatment at the center. Ronnie began by taking substitute drugs to help him break his cocaine habit. It took sixteen days of anger, sweat, convulsions, and sleepless nights before he was free enough to enter into the counseling part of the therapy.

On the sixteenth day, he rose from bed and walked to the therapy counseling room. As he entered, he was surprised to see a dozen other patients gathered for group therapy. Immediately the others began clapping, and Ronnie turned and ran back to his room. He was angry. These people were making fun of him, and he wanted nothing to do with such fools and losers.

The counselor came into his room to persuade him to return to the group. "Are you nuts?" Ronnie replied. "I paid $12,000, and I do not want to tell my story to a bunch of misguided lunatics who I have no desire to become friends with. For that kind of money, I expect a personal counselor."

He would not return to the therapy group, so in short order the entire group marched into his bedroom. Finally Ronnie cautiously acquiesced, and before long the group was in heavy conversation recounting their personal war stories and their new hope for a better life.

One night, as Ronnie was awakened from a deep sleep, he received a life-changing, heavenly vision. Strangers may not appreciate such stories, but they are very real for those who are so blessed to receive them. They become vital monuments and stabilizing touch points of faith on life's tenuous journey. Ronnie's room was suddenly flooded with a brilliant light, and a bright, white cloud hid everything from view. Standing there, in the middle of it, was Jesus. He was dressed in a pale, blue robe with a white sash tied around his waist. His arms were stretched out to Ronnie, as if he were welcoming him. He never spoke, and Ronnie didn't either, but something happened that night that was undeniable and inescapable. Ronnie received the Lord, just as the Lord was receiving him.

He did not share the vision with anyone at first, fearing that it was just a hallucination brought on by his many years of drug abuse. Maybe they would say he was crazy. After three days, the encounter continued to captivate his thoughts, and he gave way and cautiously shared it with one of the doctors. "You've had a religious experience," the doctor responded. "If it helps, you better hang on to it."

Ronnie phoned home and asked Clarice to bring him a Bible, because there was none to be found at the rehab center. He also went to Alcoholics Anonymous, and they told him there was a higher power. Before now he was not sure how things had changed, but he was certain there was a higher power, and it was Jesus, the God of the Bible. He should have died long ago and would have except for God. How could he not believe in a higher power?

To his surprise, Ronnie was put in charge of the therapy classes, and when he received the Bible from Clarice, even more wonderful things began to happen to him. He would ask the Lord for direction, counsel, or answers to his many questions. Then he would open his Bible and put his finger down on a verse, and miraculously the answer would be before him, right there in the writings of scripture. It was supernatural. When Clarice came to visit, Ronnie began to share with her how the Lord had begun speaking to him, and he demonstrated his new blessing before her eyes. "I have been a Christian for three years," Clarice retorted with mild frustration, "but God has never spoken to me so clearly."

Ronnie gently changed the subject. "I will go to church with you when I get out of here," he said, "but not to that crazy church that you attend. Those people are over the edge, and I don't want to be associated with that kind of strangeness."

Little did he realize that he was well on his way to living a life that could not be explained by those looking in from the outside. One day, people might call him crazy. "Wherever you want to go will be fine with me," Clarice responded. "I am just happy to hear you say that you will go to church."

When Sunday came Ronnie suggested that just this once they could go to Brunswick Christian Center, the crazy church that Clarice had learned to call her own. She was amazed and thankful but wondered how Ronnie would respond to her faith-filled, somewhat wild, charismatic church family. They sat at the back. The worship began, and people were singing loudly, lifting their hands, and dancing at the front. Clarice had her eyes closed, partly because she was worshiping the Lord, but also because she did not want to see Ronnie's reaction to this less than traditional meeting. Suddenly a tap on her shoulder startled her, and she turned to see the friend behind her pointing toward the front of the church. There was her Ronnie on his knees at the altar, and the pastor was praying with him. Ronnie knew he had already given his life to the Lord Jesus, but he wanted to make a public profession of his faith.

From the moment that Clarice surrendered her life to Christ, her physical condition got better. One month after Ronnie became a Christian, Clarice was healed. All of her organs functioned as they should, and she experienced no more fainting spells.

Some of the members of Brunswick Christian Center branched out and planted a new church congregation. It was called East Side World Outreach Church, and that became the Holdens' church from then till now. This church family would prove more important to them than they could have imagined. A season of unparalleled warfare was on its way, and it would hit them like an avalanche, like a mountain crashing down upon them. The cold, black cloud of death had focused all its energies on annihilating them, and it would come suddenly, at an appointed time, when they would be caught off guard. A time bomb, filled with evil, was ticking away, and it would explode in their faces, releasing such pent-up vile, sent to kill. Who could be ready for such a dark day, and what would be the outcome?

It was this church—its teachings and its training—that would equip them with the tools to stand and fight in the day of battle. The monumental is often hidden in the mundane, and church life is sometimes like that. We do not know how valuable our weekly instruction may prove to be until it is tested to the very limit. The Holdens had no idea of the intense trauma before them or the value of this church family. For now, they would be loved, learn the ways of the Lord, and wait, without warning, for the insidious to come.

Chapter 3

Lethal Force

C larice would just be gone for a few days. Island Breezes, her trendy, up-scale clothing boutique, required the personal touch. She had a flare—no, a gift—for choosing color, style, and fashion, and she personally hand-picked every piece of clothing in the store. She acquired the finest clothes from California, Miami, Dallas, Atlanta, and Las Vegas, but the best buyers were in New York, and if her business was to draw proper attention, she had to reach far beyond the humble homespun of North Carolina. She was a well-tuned businesswoman, and now that her life and marriage were focused on serving God, everything was booming.

Ronnie was so dramatically different from those early days that one would think he was another person. He became a sold-out Christian, telling the story of God's love to any who would lend an ear. He was a zealous church worker, and side-by-side with Clarice, he helped everyone he could, as God directed him. He and Clarice were diligent, hard-working, kind-hearted people, and almost everyone loved them. Ronnie's restaurant had made the necessary changes to become one of the most prominent seafood spots in the region, and the stains of a ruined life were far behind him. Failure had been replaced by success, and success was hard-pressed to keep up with blessings and abundance. They had two yachts, had owned four planes, and their estate was like one of the designer homes in Southern Living magazine. All of Ronnie's youthful aspirations and dreams had come true—not by his own hand and not in his own way, but by God's grace, in God's way. He loved the life that heaven now afforded him.

Only God can accurately answer the "whys" of life. Tragedy, disappointment, and pain come to most at sometime or another, and no one is quite prepared for that kind of interruption. Sinners and saints, rich and poor, the worst and the very best are all subject to the trials and traumas of life, and it is humbling to realize that nothing and no one are beyond the reach of collapse. Herein lies the real test of our fabric, and those who put their trust in God may prove his power and feel his faithful hand.

Clarice was still away, and Ronnie had closed the restaurant after a faithful evening of fine service. Friendly customers had once again lined up outside waiting to enjoy the fare and fellowship of Twin Lakes. On Sundays at this time of the year, the restaurant was always full, and the din of people talking and laughing and having a good time was part of the personal pleasure and fulfillment that Ronnie gained from the business. It was 10 p.m., and one by one the customers had all left, and Ronnie was ready to do the same. The clean-up crew would linger, but he was out the door, well-satisfied with another day of hard work and good profits.

The stars and moon were partly shielded by scattered cloud cover, and the light shifted from gray to pitch black and back to gray again as the scroll of heaven rolled open over the Carolina shores. The night of May 7, 2000, seemed no different from any other balmy, spring night in the South. There was a quiet pause in the air like the still before the storm, as is common when the unexpected happens. Surprise waits around the bend and then comes upon us with a flash, and in a moment, nothing is the same anymore.

It was a young man, perhaps very similar to whom Ronnie

used to be, drowning his sorrows in party and drink until he became intoxicated and lost all sense of reason and judgment. Later the autopsy revealed his blood-alcohol level was 28 percent, and in his condition, it was amazing that he could even drive— but he did. Ronnie was just two miles from home and a restful night when the man failed to stop at a stop sign, and his truck came barreling like a runaway train through the intersection. He was swerving from left to right, almost leaving the road on this side, then on the other side, at an estimated speed of eighty mph. His pickup truck smashed into Ronnie's SUV at a perfect ninety-degree angle, and he T-boned the driver's side door with such unbelievable force that Ronnie's seatbelt broke loose, and Ronnie was ejected through the passenger's side window. The glass shattered, and Ronnie shot through the air and hit the ground like a bouncing bolder crashing down the side of a mountain. The vehicle flew off the road, leveling a fire hydrant and a telephone pole. These slowed the speed of Ronnie's SUV but not enough to stop it. The vehicle flipped into a roll, turning side over side along the exact trajectory path that Ronnie's twisted body had taken. A God-fearing person might believe it was an angel who raised his hand and stayed the truck. It had turned over and over and ended up on its side teetering just two feet from Ronnie's unconscious body. Any additional momentum would have landed it directly on Ronnie.

The impact that dumped its residual mess on the front lawn shook the entire house across the street, and twenty-eight-year-old Paul jumped from his chair and ran from the house to see what had happened. The property across the road had become a catch basin for shattered and torn parts, and there before him was the limp and twisted body of a man. The driver of the pickup was dead, and Ronnie was so bloodied that Paul did not recognize him, even though he knew him. Paul raced back into the house, called 911, and brought a blanket to cover Ronnie's body, which was now in severe shock.

Suddenly Ronnie came to and opened his eyes. That's when Paul recognized him. Ronnie tried to move, but Paul told him to remain absolutely still. Then all became quiet as Paul knelt by Ronnie's side and prayed earnestly until the paramedics arrived.

Clarice was in New York with Kelly Cobb and Kim Kidd, fellow clothing store owners. They were business acquaintances, but they cared for each other like sisters. Immediately they dropped the business at hand to accompany Clarice. They boarded the first available plane, flew into Wilmington, and arrived at the New Hanover Regional Medical Center at 9:30 the next morning. Pastors Bobby and Jane Causey, along with Sandy Pigott, Barbara Campbell, and other loyal friends, were already there in the waiting room. They had come to support Clarice and to pray for God's covering and protection over Ronnie. He was in the Intensive Care Unit, and Clarice went in to see him. He was still in trauma, but the nurses had cleaned him up. Except for a few minor cuts on his face, he appeared quite normal. "He doesn't look that bad," she thought to herself. "I expected much worse."

Ronnie had broken his neck in two places, his pelvis was broken, his knee was shattered, and his left leg was fractured in fifteen places. The doctors had placed a temporary brace around his neck and were preparing to fit him with a medical halo. They would worry about his leg later. It was not a vital factor, and the MRI had not yet revealed any major internal problems. What they did not detect would prove to be their nightmare, because Ronnie's entire torso had been severely accosted, and his abdomen was experiencing silent, invasive trauma.

The doctors did not know it, but Ronnie's liver, spleen, kidneys, and intestines were torn and his own gastric poisons were seeping from his intestines into his abdominal cavity. Ronnie was quiet and still, and to all who saw him, it appeared that he was out of danger. Clarice was blessed to see that although his condition was bad, it was not that bad. He was alive, and the worst was over. Now he could get better. She would just brace herself, and God and these fine doctors would mend her husband's body. He was in the best place he could possibly be, receiving the very best care, and everything would turn out fine. She took a deep breath and returned to the warm consolation of her friends.

She had no way of knowing, but the real battle for Ronnie's life was still before her. Clarice was unaware of the carefully crafted, demonic conspiracy that targeted her husband. It would come nevertheless, one announcement of trouble after another. It was an all-out attack on his life. The attack would only intensify, but Clarice would learn to fight. In time, she would realize her desperate challenge. It would become clear; she must identify and deploy every weapon, strategy, and army she could muster until heaven triumphed and hell was halted. Not many could fight this battle and win, but Clarice and her friends were about to discover new horizons. They would dare fight with every possible weapon that God would lay before them.

Chapter 4

Death Lays Claim

The paranoia over Ronnie's health calmed and finally faded as matters appeared well in hand, and a routine for systematic care and recovery began to fall into place. He was talking, or at least trying to. Most of it, however, resembled the loose ends of unfinished sentences and weak unsupported words that made little sense. He was tired, and the accident had taken so much out of him that he did well to stay awake.

Clarice humored him. Her facial expressions shifted from a whimsical grimace, to a managed smile, depending on whether or not someone was looking. She was still dealing with the emotions of nearly losing her husband, but she rose above those feelings to show strength to others, especially Ronnie. When his weary eyelids lifted, even slightly, she bent in toward him and smiled. Then she would whisper, "I love you, dear. You're going to be all right honey."

Ronnie remembered none of this. In fact he wouldn't remember an entire month of his life following the accident. Nurses and doctors took turns evaluating and prescribing the next stage of treatment, according to their areas of expertise. Ronnie needed so much work, and they did their best to prioritize the vital and expedite appropriate care consistent with their most urgent concerns. Hospitals are huge cities of information, accumulated expertise, machines, and manpower that diversify to cover countless health needs. The resources of this hospital were now available to Ronnie.

Friends came often in those early days, and every time Clarice left intensive care to check the waiting room, a new group of church folk and family had assembled. They would chat, listen to the latest update from Clarice, and pray. Although she was thankful for the support, this was tiring for Clarice, who hadn't had a good night's sleep for days. She had found a less than comfortable spot on the waiting room sofa to nap through the nights. It was a turquoise blue, leatherette sofa, typical for many hospital waiting rooms. It was not a full-size couch, and it was worn and slightly dog-eared, but it would serve as a bed for the next month or so. She simply laid a sheet over it and went to sleep. No one could persuade her to leave the hospital, and she did not complain.

By Monday night, a halo was dully fitted on Ronnie's head, neck, and shoulders. Metal bands, bars, and bolts circling his head and caressing his shoulders made him appear more like Frankenstein than the sweet Ronnie that everyone knew. While he appeared stable, Ronnie did not seem happy or peaceful. His face was gaunt and ashen, and the still-visible cuts added to his haunting appearance.

By Wednesday, the orthopedic surgeon, Dr. Sutton, was preparing to operate on Ronnie's leg. They would not render him unconscious for the operation because of the halo and decided to administer a spinal instead. This would anesthetize his lower body and, although he would still be awake, he would not feel pain. They wheeled Ronnie into the operating room for the somewhat delicate spinal injection, and Clarice returned to Sandy and Barbara Campbell in the waiting room.

The waiting room fellowship was light and cheery, and Clarice was glad to be with friends. She hoped the conversation would distract her thoughts from Ronnie's health for a few minutes. It was difficult, because she found her mind drifting from the waiting room talk back to Ronnie's room. Then her nephew told a story that captured her attention. His eight-year-old son was at Vacation Bible School and asked a friend if he had seen the neat picture of Jesus on the wall. The friend asked if Jesus, in the picture, had a halo. He quickly responded, "No, Jesus doesn't have a halo, but my uncle has one."

Before the story was properly finished, the levity was cut short. Dr. Sutton entered the room with concern written on his face. He led Clarice to a slightly more private place out in the hall. "Ronnie has reacted to our attempts of administering the spinal," he reported, "When we bent him over to give him the needle, he became violent. I don't know how to explain it to you, Mrs. Holden. He simply went berserk. He started fighting, and even in his condition, he is very strong. He thinks we are trying to kill him." He paused and gently guided Clarice closer to the wall as a group of doctors and visitors passed by. "I am sorry, but we had to stop the procedure. At this point, Mrs. Holden, I am not sure what is happening. We are trying to get him under control. I'm sorry, but we will have to reevaluate his situation before we decide what we should do."

He looked Clarice in the eyes, squeezed her hand tenderly, and offered a consoling nod. There was nothing more he could say, no added comfort he could give that would lighten the news, and he let go of her hand and quietly walked away. Clarice was confused. Only minutes before he seemed fine. She entered Ronnie's room, and it was clear that he had been traumatized. Anxiety was all over him. He was restless, and his face was still red and flushed from the ordeal he had just encountered. The medication began taking effect, Ronnie fell asleep, and Clarice was left all alone.

Time seemed to stand still, and Clarice was not sure how long it was before a second doctor called her from the room. He was a neurologist and had been involved with Ronnie since he was admitted. He took a more direct approach. "It is what we have feared from the beginning but did not want to jump to conclusions," he said firmly. "Mrs. Holden, we think Ronnie has brain trauma. We have reason to believe that Ronnie incurred serious brain damage from the accident, and it may be irreparable. We cannot say for sure without further tests, but his irrational behavior and his slurred speech and slow cognitive responses point to the possibility of brain damage. His actions today seem only to further substantiate the prognosis. I am sorry Mrs. Holden, but I feel it is best to be upfront with you. It is best that you are prepared."

A new fist of fear hit Clarice like a prizefighter connecting with a blow that came up from the floor. A dizzy kind of numbness shook her soul. She began to feel distant and detached as if she should lay her hopes aside and stop fighting. She was tired and was tempted to give in but suddenly something rose within her, and she began punching back with the best her tired soul could manage. She was shaking her head, and her mouth was moving, but no sound was coming out as she returned to the waiting room. Her friends hastened around her as she broke through the haze and blurted, "No! No! I will not believe it. They say he has brain damage. I refuse those words." She raised her voice, "It's just not true. No way, absolutely not. He does not have brain damage."

She was ranting and pacing around the waiting room waving her arms. Her friends were caught off guard and for a moment did not know how to respond. Attempts at comfort and consolation seemed empty. Then they sat Clarice down, laid their hands on her, and began to pray.

Sandy was more than a friend. She was the church administrator, and she organized a prayer vigil. Many people in the church volunteered to take a prayer watch. Continuous prayer, from one member or another in the church family, did not stop for the next month. Someone from the church would be praying for Ronnie night and day, but for now it seemed to have no good effect. Everything became dark, and Ronnie got worse.

One night Clarice fell asleep in the chair in Ronnie's room and woke suddenly to see Ronnie standing beside his bed. It should not have been possible, because his shattered leg had not yet been worked on. Ronnie, as disorientated as he was, was determined to escape from the hospital. He was in pain and believed they were trying to kill him. Immediately a male nurse rushed into the room and forced Ronnie back to bed. During the next few hours he became more agitated and irrational. He kept pulling the feeding tubes from his nose and the monitoring wires from his body. The nurses were unable to manage the situation, and finally they were forced to tie Ronnie's hands to the bed.

"This is not my Ronnie," declared Clarice. "Something is really wrong here." She asked the doctors for another MRI, but Ronnie had received one when he came in, and it had revealed nothing. Besides that, an MRI was much more complicated now because of his halo. They would have to give special care and added precautions to undergo an MRI at this point, and the doctors assumed that Ronnie's panic and violent activity was brought on by brain damage. They talked with Clarice and explained why her request was not reasonable.

Sunday morning was Mother's Day, and most of America was filled with special church celebrations, gratitude for moms, and lively preparations for festive meals, but not in Ronnie Holden's room at New Hanover Regional. There was no merriment here. Barry Holden, Ronnie's nephew, had come to be with Ronnie, but Ronnie was in no condition for visitors. Clarice was irate. She vented her unbridled anguish on the stocky but kind-hearted male nurse in attendance. Today the entire hospital was short-staffed, and the nurse was trying to explain the situation. He was not at all insensitive, but many patients suffer trauma in the hospital. He would do his best to calm Ronnie. He would even sedate him, but this was not the day to find a lot of help. "I'm sorry, Mrs. Holden, but I can't get a doctor in here this morning," he responded. "Maybe later in the day one of the doctors will be available. I am sure they will be coming in."

Clarice wouldn't hear of it. "I want the names of everyone in charge," she fired back. "Don't tell me no doctor can come." She was yelling. She was adamant. It was obvious to her that Ronnie was in desperate and dire distress. She wanted immediate action and "no" was not an option; she refused to be placated. What was wrong with these people? Were they just going to let Ronnie die? Didn't anyone care? What is a hospital for? Who in this hospital was standing with her? She had taken all that she could, and in a sense, she became an amplifier that drew serious attention to Ronnie's condition. The nurse assessed the situation, came into agreement with her, and quickly took the matter in hand. Determined to do his job well, he picked up the phone and called down to the emergency ward. He was on the phone for some time, and Clarice caught the gist of his conversation. "If someone doesn't come up here," finally raising his impassioned voice to the receptionist, "Mrs. Holden is going to unleash the gates of hell on this place. There must be some doctor who can break away and get up here." When he heard that Dr. Maxwell was on duty he asked to speak directly with him.

That's when Dr. Maxwell and Clarice met for the first time. He was the chief trauma surgeon at the hospital and on this busy morning with only a skeleton crew available, he was giving hands-on treatment as well as overseeing all the trauma patients at the triage center. After hearing of Ronnie's condition, he rushed to see him.

He was an older man, sixty plus, very distinguished and well-seasoned in his profession. He was a tall, six-foot-three drink of cold water with a thin build and a face that resembled an eagle. It suited his character, for he appeared to gaze down from lofty heights upon his quarry, and his eyes seemed to search out and look right through a matter. He was strictly a rules man—all business, with no time for joking. The staff nicknamed him Moses, not because of any religious convictions, but because he was stern and everyone listened when he spoke. Dr. Maxwell lectured at the hospital and was responsible for the training of all trauma interns. No one pushed this man around. He was authoritative, confident, and not easily challenged, but after spending a moment with Ronnie, he ordered an immediate MRI. Because the hospital was so short-staffed, Clarice and Barry struggled together with the nurse to get Ronnie onto the table for his MRI. They had done all they could, and they waited anxiously for the results.

Before long, Dr. Maxwell came running down the hall toward Clarice. "Mrs. Holden," he said, "we must do an emergency operation now. Your husband is dying. His intestines are open, and infection has filled his body. He is septic."

Clarice was angry. She didn't trust this doctor, or for that matter anyone in the hospital. She was afraid that a wrong decision would kill Ronnie. She agreed to call a doctor whom she knew and trusted, her good friend Dr. Herb Snider. After hearing Dr. Maxwell, he urged Clarice to take his advice.

In no time, Ronnie was on the operating table, and the doctors were fighting for his life. They worked on him for seven hours, stitching up his intestines and cautiously washing the infection from his body. It was an arduous task because everything was swollen, and the poison from his intestines had spread to every possible corner and crevice in his abdominal cavity. Fifty-five pints of saline solution were used to wash him, but Ronnie's organs were septic, and he was in a mess. His kidneys were torn, his spleen was damaged, and his liver was ripped, greatly enlarged, and full of infection. The panic that erupted when they bent him over for the spinal was now understandable. His erratic and irritable behavior during the past few days was the desperate attempt of a man struggling for life.

The operation seemed to be too little, too late. When the ordeal ended, Dr. Maxwell emerged from the operating room and met Clarice. He sat before her. His mask and goggles left deep, red creases on his wrinkled face, and his light green head covering was still on his head as he lifted his heavy eyes toward her. She noticed dark circles below them and saw his soiled soul, as if it were uncovered and fully exposed. He had the look of a battle-weary soldier returning from war with the awful smell of the battlefield lingering on his clothes. "Mrs. Holden, I do not have good news for you," he began. "Ronnie's body has suffered massive violation from infection. Peritonitis has spread through his entire abdomen and affected all of his internal organs. Forgive me for being so graphic, but his body is like rotting flesh. His organs are extremely swollen with infection. They are so extended, Mrs. Holden, that it is literally impossible to put them back into his body. His abdomen remains open, and we cannot close him. We have placed damp gauze over his body cavity. We did the best we could, Mrs. Holden. He has a colostomy and is on a ventilator, and he is in a coma. Mrs. Holden I can't promise you that he will make it through the night. Truthfully, I don't think he will live for another three hours. I'm sorry, Mrs. Holden, we have done all that we can."

With that, he stood to his feet and was about to leave when Clarice rose as well. "Dr. Maxwell," she whispered, as tears filled her eyes and a trembling overtook her voice, "I don't know you, and you don't know me, but I am a woman of faith, and I'm going to pray and ask God to give you wisdom to do what is right so that Ronnie can get better. One thing I need, Dr. Maxwell, I need you to come into agreement with me, for Ronnie's life."

"Mrs. Holden," he responded, "I cannot agree with you for Ronnie. I am sorry there is nothing I can do. You may page me if you need to find me. I am sorry."

With that he turned abruptly and walked off to find some space and attend his own matters. It was Mother's Day, and he had missed it. So had Clarice. Ronnie's mother was eighty-three and unaware of her youngest son's condition. She was frail and could not have endured the traumatic news of her son's accident, and so the matter was hidden from her. Ronnie was still her baby, but for some reason he was not with her on this Mother's Day.

Mother's Day or not, a crowd of people was in the waiting room to hear the report. Clarice did what she could, but Pastor Jane took one look at her and said, "You need to be alone dear." Clarice was thankful as the pastor led her down the hall to the tiny hospital chapel and closed the door behind her. She fell to her knees and let go of all her inhibitions. Clarice cried out to God; she fell facedown, prostrate on the carpet weeping uncontrollably, pleading with the Lord Jesus for mercy. She cried for a miracle. More than an hour passed before she slowed enough to hear herself think. She found herself lying silent, listening for the voice of God. She heard nothing but felt a still peace come over her. She noticed the chapel around her. It was dead quiet and dimly lit, but it had become a precious closet of prayer. She rose with new strength in her spirit.

Slowly Clarice stepped out of the chapel into the brightness of the hospital hallway and almost bumped into Dr. Maxwell, who was startled by her sudden appearance. Without forethought, she touched his shoulder, and out of respect, Dr. Maxwell did not flinch or step back. "Dr. Maxwell," she said with gentle force, "I really, really need you to come into agreement with me for Ronnie's recovery."

She was now reaching up, holding both his shoulders, and without realizing what she was doing, she began to shake him softly. Her tender, impassioned words came again, "I know, that I know doctor, that God is going to give you wisdom. Please, come into agreement with me for Ronnie's life."

Reason was not abandoned, but something touched the doctor's heart as well as his mind, and he yielded. It was as if the fear of God came over him. He wrestled with what he knew academically and what he knew of faith and how that had helped many patients. This situation, however, was beyond that, and yet he heard himself speaking the unexpected, "Mrs. Holden, I will come into agreement with you. I will believe for Ronnie's life."

As if her personal dignity was unimportant, Clarice continued, bolder than ever. "I need your permission, Doctor, for some things. I need complete access to Ronnie, twenty-four hours a day. I promise I will not get in the way. I need to be at all the meetings where the doctors are discussing his situation. I need to know all the doctors' names and the names of the nurses, and if there is a shift change, I need to know the names of the new nurses. I need to know what is happening right now. I need specifics. I need to know what is needed to get through this night."

For a few seconds everything was quiet. Dr. Maxwell stepped back to regain his position and decorum. He looked at Clarice with a strange mixture of strength and humility. Somehow he put protocol and professional procedure aside and agreed with her requests and told her all he could. "Ronnie has a raging fever, and we have called in the infectious disease doctor. Ronnie is in a coma and is slipping away. Right now, Mrs. Holden, we just need to get through the night. You pray, and we will do whatever we possibly can." Clarice and her friends spent the night in desperate supplication. They stayed on their knees, and it was not quiet in the waiting room. How they prayed! How they interceded! They found their way through their fears, past the words of men, and beyond the reach of demonic schemes, into God's throne room. They found their way to the Ancient of Days and discovered the mercy seat of heaven and the altar of incense. They implored the Lord to send his angels. Heaven heard, and when the sun rose in the morning to wash the night from all its evil, Ronnie was still alive.

Chapter 5

The Warrior

Equal to the demonic level of chaos, God gave to Clarice and her friends a level of heaven-sent strategy. Satan had attacked, but the Spirit of the Lord was lifting up his battle flag, his standard against Satan, and Clarice was the standard bearer. She charged headlong at the enemy, prepared, if necessary, for personal wounding and even to be shot down in the fray, but the angel of the Lord watched over her. It was her focused, even reckless abandonment that brought her so far, against such odds. Some would say that Clarice fit the old adage—she charged in where angels feared to tread. But God seemed to charge in with her. He covered her and gave her just enough ammunition to stay one step ahead of her husband's attacker. The night was over and Ronnie was alive, but it was still early days in the war. Clarice was learning fast. She was experiencing on-the-job training, although training was the furthest thing from her mind. Saving Ronnie's life was all she thought of, and she refused to let go.

A spectator might have thought that Clarice was grasping at hollow straws and reaching for empty hope with any crazy thought that came to mind. No, what was happening was not chance, and her clumsy tactics were not irrational, whimsical, or crazy. She was being coached by the Holy Spirit. Clarice knew that her battle was not exclusively against the natural laws of flesh and blood. It was more than that; it was spiritual. She was fighting demon spirits who had gained entry by some unknown means, and she knew she must fight a spiritual battle with spiritual weapons. This was way off the map of medical understanding. It was a fight for faith itself, mountain-moving faith. Where could this kind of faith be found? Not in a book or in the strength or skills of this hospital and its staff, although the medical team had a critical and essential role to play. No, this kind of faith was not found there. It was in her heart. God had put it there, for he alone is the source of that kind of faith.

It is amazing how many voices can speak so many things on the same matter. Doctors, nurses, friends, relatives, acquaintances, strangers, reason, conscience, hopes, fears, and dark demons were all speaking. All their words were powerful, some meant for good and some for evil and destruction. Clarice had to deal with the voices. This tactic was for herself, her friends, the medical team, and for Ronnie, who was still in a coma. Her strategy was spun instinctively. Dealing with the negative voices was a necessary maneuver.

The doctors and nurses were amazed that Ronnie was alive on Monday morning, and some of them were beginning to understand that a power greater than modern medicine was at work. Ronnie's temperature was 107 degrees, and the battle for his life was violent. They had wrapped cooling blankets around him and stacked bags of ice against his body to do whatever they could to bring his temperature down. A ventilator and other life support systems were keeping him alive. He was unable to breath on his own, and they were monitoring every vital organ and bodily function.

Within days his kidneys stopped working, and his liver was not able to handle the huge amount of toxins in his body. Because there was insufficient output, he quickly became jaundiced. Ronnie had fourteen doctors working on him. Twenty-four tubes, wires, and intravenous ports were going in and out of his body. If one could see beyond the maze of wirers and past the halo to find his face, they would see skin that now looked old, leathery, and yellow. His ghoulish, Frankenstein look was growing darker as his medical condition grew worse.

Then Ronnie's blood pressure bottomed out. His veins were collapsing, and his heart stopped. It was a frantic moment with doctors yelling, making lightning-quick decisions, and moving with great skill and speed. They were right on it, and they jolted Ronnie back to life. They revived him, but Ronnie needed one rescue after another, and he seemed to be beyond hope. Every vital system in his body was weakening, failing, and shutting down. Ronnie was hanging on the edge of life, in a coma, with his belly wide open. He could die at any moment; in fact he was now well overdue. He was living on nothing but miracle time.

Clarice and all who visited Ronnie were required to scrub and dress in a hospital gown. They had to wear rubber gloves and a facemask, because Ronnie's open belly was subject to further infection. Visiting was an involved procedure, but Clarice came into his room as often as possible. She positioned herself in an appropriate place, so as not to get in the way, then she would look at Ronnie and say, "Doesn't he look great today?"

At first, the doctors were taken back. They knew he was more dead than alive. They would glance at Clarice and wonder how in this world she was coping with her husband's crisis. They could not help but notice a frail, all but invisible smile, hiding in the depths of her eyes. Whether they agreed with her or not, they admired this woman and wondered what they would do if they were in her position. Would they be so positive if they were in her situation? Surely it would be wrong to try to persuade her not to be positive. At any rate, it did not appear that she would listen. Their words of educated reason, if negative, would not be received by this woman of faith. So in a controlled sort of way, they nodded and smiled as if to pretend they agreed with her. After all, Ronnie was still alive.

As soon as she could, Clarice fit the headphones of a CD

player through the halo and onto Ronnie's head. He was in a coma, but she wanted the word of God to go into Ronnie's unconscious mind. She had found a recording of healing scriptures that was sent to them by Pastors J.B. and Susan Whitfield. There was no preaching or exhortation of any kind on the CD, just Bible verses that spoke of God's healing power. She played it as often as possible, night and day, and checked the player regularly to see if the batteries needed changing. Clarice had a TV in the room with Trinity Broadcasting Network (TBN), a Christian station, set on low volume, and no one dared change the channel. When no one else was in the room, she and Sandy would stop the CD player and read healing scriptures to Ronnie from his bedside, and they would sing. They only sang one song. They sang it to Ronnie. They felt in their hearts that his spirit, if not his mind, could hear them, and faith would somehow rise within him. They sang the song over and over and over again. They called it "The Healing Song," and although it was simple, they believed it was ministering strength and providing a pathway of life to Ronnie.

> He is the God that healeth thee,
> He is the Lord my healer,
> He sent his Word and healed my disease,
> He is the Lord my healer.

With all of this spiritual activity, Ronnie's room was filled with faith. Words of faith, the hearing of faith, prayers of faith, thoughts of faith, and songs of faith were the order of the day, and Clarice was determined to keep it that way.

Outside of the hospital, faith had been emphasized as well. East Side Church increased their prayer and fasting efforts, and a sign was posted on the main drag in downtown Shallotte, which read, "Pray for Ronnie Holden." Literally, thousands of people had been contacted across the country through the network of churches, ministries, and friends, and a small multitude of Christians were actively praying for Ronnie to get better. Clarice could feel the strength of their unified intercession.

Clarice stepped away from Ronnie's room for a break and entered the waiting room to find a small crowd of acquaintances, friends, and well-wishers. A mixture of relatives and church people, Christians and non-Christians were there. Everyone wanted to see Ronnie pull through, but there was a tense feeling in the air. The word on Ronnie's condition was out, and it gave no hope for those who had little or no faith. Some were quietly sobbing and wringing their hands with a hopeless feeling of loss. Sorrow and grieving were already well-established in the minds of some, because they expected that Ronnie would not make it. This was not helping Ronnie.

Suddenly Clarice lifted her voice in a gentle but stern rebuke. "This is a time for faith," she declared in a manner not unlike a firm-handed preacher pleading with his flock. "Ronnie is going to get better. Right now he needs people who stand in faith. I don't want to see tears, and I don't want to hear doom and gloom. In fact, no one can go in to see Ronnie unless they are willing to believe that Ronnie will be healed. I won't let anyone see him unless they can believe for his recovery. From now on there must be positive agreement. Everyone must have faith for Ronnie."

This may have rubbed some individuals the wrong way, but she did not care. She was not going to be political. Her Ronnie's life was all that mattered. The weeping stopped, and folks pulled themselves together. Even the non-Christians in the room agreed to believe for Ronnie's recovery, and some hearts that had been closed to God for a long time began to open again. God was at work doing more that just watching over Ronnie. Many people were drawn to the hospital because they cared, and as a result their hearts were being touched by the testimony of God's people and the constant miracles that were showing up every day.

The hospital had become a holy place. God was showing his power in an unusual way, and it was clearly recognizable for any who had eyes to see.

Life and death lay in delicate balance, and at any moment, it could tip either way. Each day brought new trials followed by frail, last-minute victories. The constant warfare was wearing Clarice thin. Demons of death came again and again, and heaven's grace quelled the attacks, but it was becoming more and more difficult to quell the secret fears that were building in Clarice.

Nights were the most difficult times, when she was tired and her reserves were low. One night, the hosts of hell mercilessly poured out their venom on her. Sandy, Barbara, Barry, or Jane always stayed with her so she was never alone, but when the lights were out and others were sleeping, the demons did their worst business. The clamor of the day had ended and the halls became empty. The doctors were gone, and many of her friends, who were always the last to leave, finally made their apologies and slipped away. Then, in the quiet with just Barbara present, Clarice stared at Ronnie. There was no response from him; a coma gives off the aura that one is already dead. All that came to her tired senses was the swishy, slushy sounds of the breathing ventilator and the sudden but infrequent beeps from the monitors.

Clarice returned to the empty waiting room in hopes of sleep, but as tired as she was, it did not come easily. Demons were scheming. They were planning to retaliate. Clarice had taken far too much ground, and the dark armies were enraged. They were waiting for an opportune moment to launch their wicked attack.

It was there, in the dark waiting room with Barbara asleep, that terror came. Quietly hovering in the upper corners of the room, the demons looked down at her. They stalked her, like wild animals. Then they came, slithering slowly. They crept down upon Clarice, like beasts silently ambushing their prey. In the gloom of an empty night, they pounced on her. They brought fear, self-pity, remorse, and anxiety. They brought panic and hopeless dread, and they came with one thought in mind—they came to crush her spirit. They wanted to shake Clarice and drive her back until they saw her wallow in worry and anxiety. They would overwhelm her mind, steal her faith, and cast her into a deep hole of despair. They were waging war, and she fell prey to their vile schemes and cunning devices.

Thinking that these thoughts were her own, she listened to the whispers of demons and started whispering their lies, back into the air. "He's not going to make it. I know it. I am really only fooling myself. I have been living in a poor man's fantasy. The doctors know. They try to tell me, but they are kind to me. Really they know the truth. Ronnie cannot get better now. He's going to die. I am so tired. I should stop this empty hope and just give up."

She even tried to be spiritual by putting forth a false humility. "Maybe I should pray and give Ronnie to God. Maybe God is wanting me to do that. Maybe he his waiting for me to come to grips with reality. I am so proud, so selfish. I am no good. This faith that everyone thinks I have—it is just a front. I don't have faith. Where is God anyway? If God were really here, why would this be so hard? I hate this. Maybe he's punishing me for my sins. Nobody knows, but God does. God is going to make me pay for my sins. I just don't care anymore. It's over. I quit. I am finished. I cannot go on anymore. I can't. I just give up."

Clarice rose to her feet, trying to shake off the torment and condemnation of her heart. Her stomach was in a knot and she felt as though she would vomit. She wandered out of the room, down the hall, and into the bathroom. It was the middle of the night, and no one was around. It was a good thing, because if anyone had seen the fit of anger and rage that came over her, they would have considered her crazy. The door closed behind her, and she leaned against the sink and looked at herself in the mirror. "Tomorrow, Clarice," she said as she spoke to herself, "you will begin to make plans for Ronnie's funeral."

Suddenly she began to wail. She cried and cried. She turned and ran at the stall behind her, pounding it with her hand again and again as frustration and anger erupted from every part of her being. "I hate this, I hate this, I hate this, I hate this," she yelled over and over again.

She was frantic, running across the room kicking and punching the doors of the stalls. Crying, screaming, yelling, she continued until utter exhaustion overtook her. She didn't care anymore. She had lost everything. Slowly she opened the door and made her way back to the sofa in the waiting room.

Clarice sobbed and sobbed as despair, fear, and self-abuse filled the room. It filled her heart and her mind. It was as though the demons had taken all the sound waves, and no other voices could be heard. They jumped her, beat her, and sifted her. Before one evil thought had finished its vile work, another would come crashing in. She could think of nothing good, for goodness had abandoned her. Panic and restlessness pressed her, pushed her, and tormented her until she thought of nothing except that which was full of fear. She became afraid of a lonely future. She thought of what would happen if Ronnie were gone, and she thought the worst. She thought of the troubles that might happen to her, and her thoughts were much worse than one could imagine.

It was then that she wanted to die just to stop the taunting and torment. She wanted to end it. She was so tired. All her strength was gone. Physical pain ripped at her stomach and squeezed her until her body ached. It felt as though all of her chronic sickness and diseases that had left her years before returned to her en masse in one dreadful attack. She tossed and turned from side to side, curled up in a ball on the couch. She sobbed and sobbed and could not stop, and no one came to her rescue.

Demons danced overhead with glee and merriment and chuckled to each other, boasting over their breakthrough victory. They had taken the night, and they knew it. Clarice was in agony, coiled in fetal position, holding her stomach. She was in unbearable pain. It seemed that it lasted all night. She did not know when it ended, because she fell asleep or blacked out. She did not know how long she slept, but it was still dark when her eyes opened again.

She lay still, not wanting to move, for the longest time. She was taking stock, remembering the evil trauma of the night. How wicked it was. How could she be dragged so low? She took note that some relief had come. In fact, she felt better, strangely refreshed, as if secret angels had snuck into the room unawares, to administer health back into her soul during the final hours of the night. Strangely, she felt the presence of God in the room, and slowly she leaned on her arm and sat up on the couch. She pulled her disheveled hair back and wiped the perspiration from her face on the side where it had rested against the leatherette sofa. She felt the deep creases on her cheek from the hard piping of the couch. Her body ached, but that was unimportant.

The room was just beginning to lighten, as a subtle glow warmed the sky beyond her window. The sun had not yet appeared, but it was coming. She could see the signs of a new day, and she felt glad to see it. "Thank you, Lord," were the first words that broke free from her crusty, dry mouth. They were groggy, unclear words, but she forced them out, for her mind had become clear. She swallowed hard, "Thank you for getting me through the night." She was glad that she was still alive. What a battle! What an awful battle! What a dreadful battle! Things looked different now. "Lord," she continued softly, "forgive me. I did not do well. I failed. Oh God, forgive me!"

She paused for a while, reflected on the night's events, then started up again, "In Jesus name, I renounce every lying word that came to me, and I renounce the evil words that I spoke last night. I reject them all. In Jesus name, I reject those wicked, demon spirits. I will have nothing to do with them. You demon spirits, I rebuke you in the name of Jesus and in his name, the name of Jesus, I command all of you to go."

She sighed deeply, as a weight that was still lingering lifted off her back and left the room. "Thank you, Lord," she continued. "Lord, I do have faith, your faith! You are my God, my Lord, and I will have no other god in my life, only you. You are my strength and my light. I will not be afraid. Lord, protect me this day. Watch over Ronnie and heal him. Oh God, please heal my Ronnie. Thank you, Lord. I love you, Jesus. There is no one like you who cares for me. Today I rededicate my life to serve you and to stand in your strength. Come, Holy Spirit, wash me and help me serve you better."

With each word, Clarice felt more of God's presence within her and all around her. It was great to feel his goodness again. Finally she stood and straightened her stiff, bent-over body. She almost lost her balance but steadied herself to regain her feet. She reached up and stretched her arms, lazily toward heaven, and she sauntered slowly, shuffling her feet as she went toward the window and leaned on the sill. The sun, although still not in sight, had cast its rays on the underside of the distant clouds, far away on the horizon. Those rays were bouncing off the clouds and reflecting into the waiting room where Clarice stood. The light became brighter, and Clarice had to squint to look full into the glowing embers on the edges of the clouds. She stared at the beauty of the red morning sky and knew that the night was finally over, and she had made it through to a brand new day.

Chapter 6

Staying in the River

Clarice walked the hall with a light-hearted step and renewed faith in her heart. Last night's encounter made her even more confident that she was in a spiritual battle and that God was with her. The demons must have been mad, because Clarice was happier than ever.

The situation in intensive care, however, had not improved, and when Dr. Maxwell arrived, he told Clarice that the infectious condition around Ronnie's organs remained hostile. His fever would not break, and they continued to pack ice around him. "Ronnie's body just cannot endure this continuous trauma," he said. "Mrs. Holden, we must try to close his abdomen. His body has been open for six days now, and it is extremely dangerous. We are taking him back to the operating room this morning. Several doctors will be assisting us, and we will do what procedures we can. Keep praying, Mrs. Holden."

She went to the chapel and prayed desperately. By late morning she felt the demonic lies closing in on her again, but she quickly repelled any notion of fear and renewed her strong grip on the Lord. Her prayers and positive confession held her to the mark, and at times she rose with loud aggressive prayer and knew that she was moving forward in the battle for faith.

At noon Ronnie, still in a coma, returned from the operating room. There was tension in the air around the nurse's station, and one could feel the disappointment. The ICU nurses knew how important the operation was, but the doctors had been unsuccessful. Ronnie's organs were still far too swollen, and they could not put them back inside his body. What they had hoped for did not happen. Clarice shook herself as if to dislodge the immediate trauma from gaining a foothold and reducing her faith level. She wanted to maintain a right mindset.

While the doctors had been working hard in the operating room, she had been at work in the chapel. She was feeling tired and hungry, so she joined Sandy and Barry for a bite of food in the cafeteria. She was deep in thought and silent prayer as she nibbled at her sandwich plate. She did not taste the food or even remember eating it, because she was in deep conversation with God. She was slowly wading out into an ever-deepening river of fellowship with the Holy Spirit. She talked with the Lord quietly, in her mind, and listened as well. She was drawing grace, faith, and strength from the Lord. Her mind was focused where it should be; it was stayed on Christ.

Suddenly she was brought back to earth. A well-dressed, white-haired lady placed her tray down on the opposite side of her table. "Do you mind if I sit with you folks?" she asked.

"Of course not," Clarice responded, trying to compose herself and be friendly. "Be our guest."

The woman was obviously many years older than Clarice, but she had kept herself well and had a proper way about her. She had a pale complexion, which was exaggerated by an all-too-powdery foundation. She had visible age spots, yet her skin looked plump and soft, and when she smiled, she acted as though she were self-conscious about her dentures.

They introduced themselves politely, and Clarice tried to engage in conversation but quickly realized that the lady's dignified outward appearance was overshadowed by a sad countenance and a heavy disposition. She was covered with grief and sorrow. She wore them like an old, oversized coat that a bag lady might wear.

She was in search of company with whom to share a cup of pity, and she was not slow in extending her chalice of hopelessness to Clarice. "I see that our husbands are both in intensive care," she whispered softly as she reached out to find a sorrowful response from the other side of the table. "It seems, I'm so sorry to say, that they are both in the same hopeless mess."

Clarice looked up at her, wondering what she would say next, and whether she could abide such talk. Her friends had not spoken a word to deflect the conversation, and Clarice was feeling uncomfortable. Already she felt the soothing waters of God's river rush away from her conscious mind, and hard, barren ground come up beneath her feet. She knew she could not allow her spirit to be knit with such a defeatist mindset and with such self-pity. Anger began to stir within her as she remembered the awful, awful night she had endured and the painful tactics the demons used against her. She was still reeling from the morning of battle over Ronnie's health. Only moments before, she had been challenged by new fears, and those emotional pressures were lingering around her soul. There was no visible response on her face, but she was boiling inside.

The woman continued on her downward path. "Their vital organs have all stopped," she said, as sorrow-filled tears began welling in the corners of her eyes. "They are already unconscious. It is really just the early stages of death. My brother John went like that. Slowly things stopped working, and then, just like that, he was gone. We have to get ready; both of them are going to die. Don't you think so?"

She would have carried on, but Clarice cut her off. She bolted to her feet and grabbed her own tray in such a rough manner that her spoon and fork fell to the floor. "I'm not having any of this," she yelled, as she bent over to pick up her fallen silverware. "I will not sit here and listen to this."

She had pushed her chair back and was moving from the table when she turned and blurted out one last soulful remark.

"You think whatever you want to, ma'am, but my husband is not going to die or anything like that. My husband is going to recover. He's going to live. I'm not having this."

Clarice moved away quickly and found a private spot on the other side of the room. She sat down quietly, but inside she was rattled and disheveled. She found it hard to finish her meal. One thought kept repeating in her mind: "I had to do what I had to do." Then she tried to forget about it. She focused on the Lord and meditated on his promises. "I can do all things through Christ who strengthens me," she said.

She was getting her thoughts back on track. She felt sorry for the older lady, but she was in survival mode, and nice feelings and proper manners would have to be put aside for now. She fought to keep herself from coming under an oppressive spirit. She had to guard what she listened to. She had to maintain her faith.

Sandy and Barry consoled the woman who had just been abandoned by Clarice. Then they politely left the table and joined Clarice. Once again, like many times on the journey, Sandy and Barry were a wonderful godsend. Clarice took the time to tell her friends all that had happened to her through the night. Their dedicated support was a necessary part of heaven's defense for Clarice. They were a real strength; more than mere friends, they were absolutely unified in spirit with Clarice. They reaffirmed her ground of faith and spoke words of life and hope.

Ronnie had not improved, and more machines were brought in to help deal with his organ failure. Clarice and Sandy were scrubbed and dressed in their hospital gowns sitting at his side. They were praying, reading, and gently proclaiming the word of God, but they had to stop often as the doctors and nurses frequented the room. Eventually a nurse asked them to leave.

Doctors pushed past, and nurses ran around his bed, fighting to stabilize his condition. The medical team worked frantically to shore up one failed system after another in Ronnie's body. They were endeavoring to rescue him from one more brush with death. Miracle after miracle kept him alive that day. Some of the nurses and doctors confessed that they had no other explanation, except it had to be God. Whether in the room or out of it, Clarice and Sandy engaged in non-stop prayer. At the same time, the doctors were involved in non-stop emergency procedures. That day, there were five occasions when the trauma escalated to the threshold of death, and Ronnie should have died—but he didn't.

Clarice and Sandy stood outside the main ICU door, quietly and fervently praying for Ronnie's life. A middle-aged lady, who was visiting a patient in the room beside Ronnie's, came toward them. She introduced herself and said, "I'm sorry that your husband is having such a battle, but I've seen you pray, and I do believe that God is with you. He is hearing and answering your prayers. Would you mind taking a moment to pray for my dad?"

Clarice and Sandy agreed to do so, because although they were set on praying for Ronnie's crisis, this did not feel like a distraction. In fact Clarice felt as though she were back in a river of God's grace, and to share his love with others seemed the most natural thing she could do. They followed the lady and prayed with enthusiasm for her dad. Word spread, and other requests came, and they responded. Soon they were moving from one intensive care bed to another like missionaries serving at some national disaster site. It seemed the more they prayed for the needs of others, the quicker their own prayers for Ronnie were answered. They were flowing in the river of God, and now the river was flowing from them to others.

At the end of the day, as the battles for Ronnie's life seemed to subside for a moment, Pastor Bobby Causey came to the hospital. Dr. Maxwell met him in the hall. "Are you here to see Ronnie Holden?" he asked.

"Well yes," Bobby replied, "but I'm going to visit a lady first."

"If she's a member of your church," the doctor continued with confidence, "I am sure she will be just fine. The way you people pray is just amazing. When you folks pray, people definitely get better."

As darkness fell and evening came, Clarice and Sandy realized they had spent the entire day in prayer, yet they did not feel as though they should stop. They were energized and geared up. They felt they had received a special anointing for prayer, and they should continue in it as long as they could, as long as the grace of God remained on them. Together they walked the hospital halls in hushed and earnest prayer. They systematically prayed a prayer of agreement at various stations in and around the building. They prayed in the waiting room, in the chapel, at the doorway to intensive care, outside the emergency ward, the prenatal ward, and outside the front doors of the hospital. These touch points became portals for the release of God's blessings and power.

The grace of God was with them. His anointing was upon them, and they experienced great authority in the Holy Spirit. Faith soared in their hearts, and it felt as though they were calling heaven, and thousands of angels were responding. Their faith was so vibrant, and they were so confident that they believed, at that moment, if Ronnie had died, by God's grace, they could have called him back to life.

The power of God had enveloped them in an altogether inexplicable peace. As they prayed into the early hours of the morning, their humanity caught up with them, and they began to tire. They stepped back from the altar of prayer, returned to the waiting room, and although their place of rest was rough and primitive, that night they slept as well as ever they had.

Chapter 7

Reinforcements

During the next week, the doctors took Ronnie to the operating room twice. Both times they failed to close up his abdomen, because his infection had not subsided. He had been in a coma for ten days; it was hard to believe that things could get worse, but they did.

Each day Ronnie faced a battle with death, and when Sandy came in at ten o'clock in the morning, Clarice was desperate. It was as though her back was against the wall, and she had nowhere to go. Ronnie's nurse had told her that the doctors had been working since early morning, but they could not stabilize his condition. Every vital organ had stopped functioning, and she could only say, "Nothing is stable. Ronnie is slipping away. I am sorry Clarice, but it does not look good. Things are very bad, dear."

The nurse walked with Clarice out into the hall, but they remained in ICU. Sandy rushed to the phone station at the far end of the corridor and phoned Bobby and Jane. "We really need reinforcements in here. It just feels like we are losing the battle. We are losing Ronnie. Can you call the praise team to come in? We are desperate. We need help as soon as possible."

Sandy returned to the frontlines to pray with Clarice. It was rough. They wept and cried. Again and again they called to God for mercy. Whenever they phoned into the nurses' station, the report was unchanged—Ronnie was fighting for his next heartbeat. The battle continued into the afternoon, and then reinforcements came. Leslie, Sue, Danette, Nelda and Pastors Bobby and Jane arrived with a boom box and some praise music. Before long the waiting room became a house of prayer and praise. They sang and worshipped with great enthusiasm. They were declaring the life of the Lord over Ronnie.

The team knew the Bible story of Jericho's walls falling at the blowing of the trumpets. The Israelites marched around the walls for seven days, and on the seventh day they blew their trumpets and shouted. The walls of their enemy came crashing down. The team pictured themselves fighting the enemies called death and infirmity in like fashion.

They remembered the story of King Jehoshaphat who sent the singers and the players out in front of the army. They were an army of musicians. They worshipped and praised the Lord and understood that the battle was not theirs, but the Lord's. As with Jericho, God Almighty came and fought for King Jehoshaphat and his army. He destroyed their enemies. They read the scripture.

> "Listen, King Jehoshaphat! ... This is what the Lord says to you: 'Do not be afraid or discouraged because of this vast army. For the battle, is not yours, but God's.... Jehoshaphat appointed men to sing to the Lord and to praise him for the splendor of his holiness as they went out at the head of the army, saying: 'Give thanks to the Lord, for his love endures forever.' As they began to sing and praise, the Lord set ambushes against the men of Ammon and Moab and Mount Seir ... and they were defeated." 2 Chronicles 20:15, 21, 22 NIV

The praise took hold of this biblical principle. They were fighting the enemies of God with worship and praise. They believed that the Lord would fight for them. His enemies were their enemies. Death is man's last enemy, and right now death was bearing down on Ronnie. They could not beat him by themselves, but God most certainly could.

They thought of Paul and Silas, the New Testament missionaries, who were taken prisoner, beaten, and put in stocks. Rather than caving in to defeat, at midnight they began to praise the Lord. They were in an impossible situation. How could they fight back? As ministers sent by God, they realized they were on assignment, doing the Lord's work, and the battle was his battle. Their military tactic was to praise him. As Paul and Silas worshipped God, he fought their battles. He sent an earthquake and broke the stocks and chains off of them and set them free. The results were unexpected. The jailor and his family saw the power of God and were converted to Christ.

The East Side worship team followed the biblical example. For a couple of hours, they lifted their hearts to heaven in powerful praise and worship. They felt God's presence and were touched by his Holy Spirit. They knew they had found a true biblical pattern, and they lined up with it. They obeyed the Lord and felt his presence, but no visible change came to Ronnie. He was dying.

Every hour through the day, Clarice called the intensive care unit, but Ronnie did not improve. His life hung by a delicate thread, and any moment the news could come that the thread had broken, and Ronnie had fallen from this life. He was only alive because of the grace of God and the hospital's life support systems, and the latter was extremely fragile and failing.

Clarice had gone for another meeting with the doctors, and Pastor Jane and Sandy decided to go to the next level. They had already used the waiting room far beyond its normal function, so they took the worship team into the chapel. They were somewhat restrained in the waiting room, but the chapel seemed more soundproof, and they thought they would cause less disturbance there. They remembered the scripture:

"The effectual, fervent prayer of a righteous man avails much."
(James 5:16)

So they went to answer the prompting of the Holy Spirit. They went to find effectual, fervent prayer, and they prayed as fervently and as effectively as they could.

In the chapel, they lifted their voices. They held nothing back but prayed with everything they had. They yelled as though no one outside of the chapel, except God, could hear them. They prayed in unity and harmony. It was as though a conductor were present leading them and giving each one her queue. Sometimes they prayed all at once, shouting into the heavens with a single voice. Other times they took turns casting a separate cry from a desperate heart, and the others would echo agreement with "amens" and "hallelujahs." The sounds coming from the room were certainly unfamiliar to most of the hospital staff at work that day. Some were absolutely convinced that something terrible was going on.

There was a great ruckus coming from the chapel, and after a while the security guard opened the door, accompanied by a police officer. They had thought that perhaps a fight had broken out. There was indeed a fight going down in the chapel, but it was not a domestic one. It was not a fight against flesh and blood. The ladies were fighting against spiritual powers of wickedness, and they were doing it with every bit of strength they had. The police officer said, "Is everything all right in here?"

"Yes officer," came a quick reply.

The officer was fine with that and closed the door. The group hardly missed a beat, but carried on praying, prophesying, pronouncing, and proclaiming, "Ronnie Holden will live. He will not die. Ronnie will recover and declare the works of the Lord. We speak it forth this day, in the name of Jesus who is King of kings and Lord of lords."

Hours passed, as though the clock were a high-speed, wind-up toy spinning round and round. The ladies moved from earth time to throne-room time. They lost all track of time. They prayed until most of what they had inside of them had expired. When they finally walked out of the chapel, they discovered that many hours had passed. There are no windows in the chapel but looking out of the front glass doors of the hospital, they saw it was dark outside. Night had come.

Most of the praise team had to rush to their homes and responsibilities. Clarice stayed in touch with ICU, but Ronnie's condition was still the same. His battle was far too intense, and it had been much too hard, for too long. The doctors had fought desperately for his life before this, but their efforts focused on one or two challenges. Now it involved many facets and factors, and each one could end Ronnie's life. The battle lasted day after day. It did not let up, and yet Ronnie did not die.

Jane stayed as long as she could but finally had to leave and attend her family. Sometime that evening Clarice's nephew arrived. Sandy was still there with Clarice, but their energy was gone, and quiet prayers now squeaked out through raspy, worn-out voices. A cold, dank spirit was blowing through the hospital. At one or two in the morning a demonic heaviness settled in and sent an evil chill over the entire intensive care unit.

The ward consisted of surgical intensive care, cardiac intensive care and trauma intensive care, and the place felt like it had become a morgue. The unit was full of patients, and everyone was in severe trauma and crisis. People were dying. Spirits of hopelessness and death were ruling over the ward. Clarice, Sandy and Barry were increasingly despondent as hopelessness and weariness enveloped them.

Despair had come over Clarice before but not during the daytime when Sandy or Barbara were with her. Despite their prayers and with all of the help that one could possibly expect from friends, Ronnie had not changed. It seemed that all that effort produced nothing. Anxiety and dread covered Clarice, and she felt absolutely empty as if she had nothing more to give.

They stood in the hall outside of ICU, just across from the elevator. They were exhausted. Sandy knew that Clarice would not sleep with Ronnie holding on to life by such a thin string, so she refrained from even suggesting that sleep would be a good idea. Then something happened. Ever so softly, as if a music conductor had just moved into place, they caught the downstroke of his baton and began to sing a frail song. One after the other, they caught on, and soon they were singing together. To a passerby, it would have sounded more like a dirge than a worship song, but it was coming up from a long way down, from the very basements of their hearts. "Thank you Jesus, thank you Jesus, thank you Jesus, thank you Jesus," was all the song consisted of.

They could hardly get the song out, but they continued singing. Suddenly, as though they shifted into another dimension, a strange feeling came over them. They looked up, and coming toward them from the far end of the corridor was a black lady. She was a cleaning lady, mopping the floor. She was still a long way off, but she kept looking up at them as she mopped. She heard their song and began singing along with them. They could not stop staring at her, and they harmonized with her and her with them in the "Thank you Jesus, thank you Jesus" song. Her face shone, and the air around her carried a feeling of goodness. The song became like a battering ram pushing and moving all the foul air out of the hallway. She was definitely mopping more than just the dirt off of the floor; she was displacing darkness. For more than a couple of minutes she came toward them, slowly doing her job. She swayed from side to side in gentle rhythm with the Jesus tune, and all the while she was singing and mopping.

When finally she arrived in front of the elevator where they were standing, the elevator beeped and the doors slid open, but no one was near the buttons. They expected someone to exit, but it was empty; no one was there. A fresh breeze, however, swept out of the elevator, and with it came a wonderful peace that flooded the hallway. All the anxiety and dread that had troubled them moments before lifted immediately, and the sweet presence of the Lord struck their faces and swept down upon them. They strained to see if they might catch a glimpse of an angel, but they could not see anything. They knew, however, that a heavenly being had entered the place.

At that moment there was a shift in the atmosphere in the intensive care unit. Every traumatic situation became stable and a quiet, and calm settled upon the nurses and patients. Clarice and Sandy could not stop talking about what had just happened. It was as if a tornado suddenly stopped dead in its tracks, and a beautiful sunny day appeared. One minute they felt totally disconnected from heaven and the presence of the Lord, and a moment later heaven had come down and surrounded them. How excited they were. How wonderful they felt.

Before retiring they prayed, "Lord refresh us as we sleep. Give us your continued strength for tomorrow and the days ahead and give us added wisdom so we might fight this battle well. Thank you for all that you have done to push back the enemy at the end of this day. No matter what has happened, you alone have the last word."

The following morning they asked about the cleaning lady, but she was nowhere to be found. None of the nurses or patients had ever seen her, and when they described her appearance to the other members of the cleaning crew, they told the two women no one like that worked at the hospital, and they must have been mistaken.

Clarice and Sandy could not discover who the cleaning lady was or where she had come from. To them, she was another miracle. She was a godsend, a spiritual soldier sent from God.

That morning, Dr. Maxwell called a special meeting. It was held in the nurses' bull pit in the intensive care unit. That is the area at the back of the nurses' station, behind the long semicircular counter. The meeting was open for anyone in ICU to see and hear, but vital decisions had to be made, so they met right there across from Ronnie's room. At least twelve doctors were present, including Dr. Clancy, Maxwell's assistant in surgery, kidney specialists, neurology and disease control doctors and others. Of course Clarice was there. "Mrs. Holden," Dr. Maxwell said, "yesterday was so difficult, and we are all amazed that we did not lose Ronnie at one point or another. His body cannot take any more of this. There is a helicopter waiting outside, and we think we should transfer him to Chapel Hill."

Chapel Hill is a university hospital, one of the largest and most respected in the country, but Clarice did not feel right about this suggestion. "What can they do there, Doctor, that you can't do here?" she asked.

"They have the best of equipment and the latest technology," he responded, "They can do tests on their machines that we might not be able to do, and their labs can evaluate things at a more advanced level. There would be risks, but I do not want Ronnie to be here and experience another day like yesterday."

"Dr. Maxwell," Clarice came back, "I am sure that people die at Chapel Hill just as they do here. But God is here with us, and he is giving you wisdom for Ronnie. I appreciate your wonderful efforts to find him the best help, but can we not be in communication with them at Chapel Hill? Can we not send them samples and data for their analysis, testing, and evaluations?"

Dr. Maxwell had mixed feelings about the transfer for many reasons. The primary one being that the move might be too hard on Ronnie; they could lose him on the journey. When Clarice asked those challenging questions and shared her disquiet, the good doctor retracted his idea. Later everyone agreed that the move probably would have killed Ronnie. In retrospect,

Clarice was even more thankful because, once again, she realized that God was one step ahead of the problem. He had given her the right questions, wisdom, and suggestions so that she might play her part at the right moment. She knew she was receiving help from God, because her participation in Ronnie's healing was well beyond her own level of skill.

Ronnie improved greatly, and the following day they wheeled him back into the operating room. His infections had subsided significantly, allowing the doctors to successfully place his organs back inside his body and stitch him up. Nineteen days had passed since Ronnie's accident. His abdomen had been open for twelve days. He was still in a coma, but the doctors were able to gather new hope. Miracles were happening.

Times like these spawn questions about unanswered prayers—why some prayers get answered and why others do not. Only God can answer such queries. Every situation is different, and there are more unknown variables than known ones in any story of trauma. God's promise for his children is clear: He will never leave them nor forsake them. (Heb. 13:5). God always shows up in some marvelous way when we diligently seek him.

Our expectations may not be fulfilled, but his always are. He invented and designed prayer for our direct contact and interaction with him. True, heartfelt prayer is therefore always powerful, instructive, and absolutely vital for the release of his blessings in our lives. He always answers prayer according to his will. The absence of prayer leaves a task unfinished, while the employment of it shakes heaven and earth.

Was the end-of-the-day breakthrough for Clarice and Ronnie due to the intense praise? Was it their prayers and the spiritual warfare she and her friends had waded through all day long that brought the victory? The answer is—most certainly. They did not see results immediately when they prayed, but eventually their expectations were met. God clearly and most decisively answered their prayers.

Hebrews 11:6 instructs us that without faith it is impossible to please God. The faith described includes an essential qualifier. We must believe that he will reward us if we diligently seek him. Clarice and friends sought him diligently, and he rewarded them, even though there was a space of time between the prayers and the reward. On one occasion, Daniel prayed for twenty-one days before he received the answer to his prayer (Dan. 10:12–14).

Jesus taught his disciples to pray with passion and persistence and to never give up. To do so, he told a very strange story.

> *"There was a judge who neither feared God nor cared about men. And there was a widow … who kept coming to him with the plea, 'Grant me justice against my adversary.' For some time he refused. But finally he said to himself, 'Even though I don't fear God or care about men, yet because this widow keeps bothering me, I will see that she gets justice, so that she won't eventually wear me out with her coming!' And the Lord said, '… And will not God bring about justice for his chosen ones, who cry out to him day and night? Will he keep putting them off? I tell you, he will see that they get justice, and quickly. However, when the Son of Man comes, will he find faith on the earth?"* Luke 18:2–8 NIV

Chapter 8

Three Angels

Ronnie Holden was in a coma for twenty-one days, the same number of days that Daniel waited for an answer to his hallmark prayer. An epic battle roared in the heavens between good and bad angels while Daniel waited for his prayers to be answered on earth. The battle was a direct result of his prayers.

That is what happened to Ronnie and the intercessors who surrounded him. He was in a coma for twenty-one days. While Clarice and her friends prayed and fought for his life, Ronnie was experiencing continuous interaction and fellowship with angels.

Angelic visitations are not unusual. Multitudes of people have experienced visits from angels at some time in their lives. The Bible instructs us to welcome strangers with kind hospitality, because many people have entertained angels without knowing it (Hebrews 13:2).

While most Christians believe the Bible stories about angels, many are skeptical about modern-day accounts of angels. God has not changed, and his angels have not become inactive. What happened in Bible times happens today as well.

Let us look at some Bible stories that involve angels. The angel Gabriel stood before Mary and announced to her the message of the incarnation. What ensued was a very thoughtful, two-way conversation.

"In the sixth month, God sent the angel Gabriel to Nazareth, a town in Galilee, to a virgin. ... The virgin's name was Mary. The angel went to her and said, 'Greetings, you who are highly favored! The Lord is with you.... Do not be afraid, Mary, you have found favor with God. You will be with child and give birth to a son, and you are to give him the name Jesus. He will be great and will be called the Son of the Most High. The Lord God will give him the throne of his father David, and he will reign over the house of Jacob forever; his kingdom will never end.' 'How will this be,' Mary asked the angel, 'since I am a virgin?' The angel answered, 'The Holy Spirit will come upon you, and the power of the Most High will overshadow you. So the holy one to be born will be called the Son of God. Even Elizabeth your relative is going to have a child in her old age, and she who was ... barren is in her sixth month. For nothing is impossible with God.' 'I am the Lord's servant,' Mary answered. 'May it be to me as you have said.' Then the angel left her." Selections from Luke 1:26–38 NIV

An angel appeared to Mary's fiancé, Joseph, as well; not in a daytime visit as with Mary, but in his dreams.

The angel said, *"Joseph son of David, do not be afraid to take Mary home as your wife, because what is conceived in her is from the Holy Spirit. She will give birth to a son, and you are to give him the name Jesus, because he will save his people from their sins."* Matt. 1:20, 21 NIV

On at least three other occasions the angel of the Lord appeared to Joseph in dreams and gave him important information and detailed instructions. Angels spoke to the Magi and appeared before the shepherds who were watching their sheep in the fields. Angels have visited many of God's children down through the centuries. They appeared to Adam, Abraham, Hagar,

Jacob, Joshua, Elisha, Daniel, Peter, Paul, John, and Jesus, to name only a few.

Hebrews 1:14 tells us:

"Are not all angels ministering spirits sent to serve those who will inherit salvation?"

And Jesus said:

"I tell you the truth, you shall see heaven open, and the angels of God ascending and descending on the Son of Man." John 1:51 NIV

Angels are not restricted to visiting God's people only during Bible times. They are sent by God to serve his people, at any time, in any land, to any tribe or people group and to every generation. We should expect them and be prepared to welcome them.

During the time of Ronnie's coma, the doctors, nurses, his relatives and friends did all they could to keep him alive. The medical team used life-support systems, intravenous drugs, and dozens of medical procedures to sustain him. They literally forced air and food into his body and drained the toxins and wastes away. They breathed for him, washed his kidneys, and kept the electrolytes and chemicals balanced in his body.

At the time, Ronnie was unaware of any of their magnificent efforts, but while the medical team was employing their skills, the spiritual team was engaging theirs. The words of faith, declarations of life, proclamations, prophesying, praise, commands against evil spirits, supplications, and petitions were as significant and as vital as any work the doctors were administering. They came into agreement with God and stayed the hands of demons and provided a landing strip for the host of heaven, for the angels to come.

Just as Ronnie did not know the efforts and hard work of the nurses, doctors, and the prayer team, they were unaware of his heavenly visitors. It was later, after he had fully come out of the coma, that he told Clarice the entire story.

There were three angels who stayed with Ronnie for the entire time that he was in the coma. They came to him in dreams when he was in the coma and appeared to him in day visions after he was revived. Ronnie was lying in his hospital bed unconscious with tubes and wires, a halo and life-support apparatus attached to his body in every conceivable place, but that is not how he saw himself, and he did not suffer or feel pain. He knew he was sick and that he was being cared for in the hospital, and he knew he was weak, but everything else was quite different. None of the life-support equipment was evident to Ronnie. He did not see himself like that. He was simply lying in the hospital bed clothed in pajamas.

In his mind, Ronnie's bed was elevated on a slant, and he was propped up, so he could see out of the window. This was not the case in the real world, but for Ronnie it was very real. Each day he looked from this hospital bed, through a full-length, floor-to-ceiling window. His vista gave him an ocean view, starting with the docks and extending far out to the beautiful blue horizon. Many small and medium-sized craft were tied up in the harbor, and most of them were colorful sailboats, although many were large, motorized vessels as well. He spent his days looking out of the window, captivated with the beauty and wonder of the sea and with the people walking and working around the marina. Ronnie thought that the hospital must have done a great deal of construction to extend their building down to the ocean. The last time he visited the hospital it was not so close to the water. In actual fact, it was four miles from the water, and the docks could not be seen from any part of it.

At first he did not realize that the three men in his room were angels. They looked like average men of average height wearing average clothes. They were kind and eager to serve, but beyond their amazing grace of character, they did not stand out as being different from normal men. In the beginning they did not talk. They hung around, read the paper, and once in a while they would look over at Ronnie. On the third day Ronnie heard a voice. It said, "I have sent my angels to watch over you." Then Ronnie knew that everything would be all right.

Each day, precisely at five o'clock in the afternoon, the angels would take him out of his room. They helped Ronnie out of bed and slowly walked with him, one holding each arm to support him. Together they made their way out of the hospital doors and down the long, grassy path to the dockside. It seemed that they wanted Ronnie to get some fresh air and much-needed exercise. They walked him along the boardwalk, across a wide gangplank, and onto a very fine sailing vessel. How it glistened and shone. The hull was a deep emerald green, and the superstructure and cabin were beige. The main body was accented with marvelous mahogany and rich-looking, well-rubbed teak trim. The boat never failed to capture Ronnie's attention and admiration. Its craftsmanship was absolutely outstanding, and Ronnie, being a seasoned boatman, appreciated the details more than a land lover might.

His visits to the boat became a daily event and such a favored routine that Ronnie looked forward to them with great anticipation. He spent every evening and the entire night in the fellowship of the angels aboard this fabulous boat. He sat in the main cabin looking out through its windows. The weather was constantly sunny with hardly a cloud in the sky, and the gulls, pelicans, and other seabirds flew around the boat often landing on the gunnels. The boat never pulled away from the shore but remained docked, as if it were stationed there just for Ronnie.

What he remembered most of those amazing nights was the outstanding food. Spread before him every evening was a banquet fit for royalty. A smorgasbord of unusual fare had been prepared meticulously, and the angels waited on him while they talked and ministered the presence of the Lord to him. The water they brought him was incredible. He was always so very thirsty, and the angels gave him water filled with crushed ice. It was so cold, and it quenched his thirst like nothing else could. He had never tasted water like this before. It was so good and so refreshing, and he drank of it again and again, and as he did it strengthened and delighted him, and he wanted more.

He was also taken aback by the massive bowls of delicious-looking fruit. There were all kinds of fruit of various sizes and shapes, but the apples appeared particularly wonderful. There were many varieties of apples, and all were unusually large and perfectly shaped and colored. One fruit that he had never seen before became his favorite treat. He never did discover exactly what it was, but it was pure white and perfectly round and plump. It was just a bit smaller than a grapefruit. When he bit into it, he thought it was the best fruit he had ever eaten. If anything came from heaven, he thought, this certainly did. One bite filled his mouth with an abundance of juice, and he had to be careful to keep it from bursting out through his lips. It was so sweet and tasty that he wanted some every night.

How he enjoyed the food, the boat, the motion of the gentle tides, and his fellowship with the angels. After a full evening of dining and wonderful fellowship, Ronnie slept on a massive king-size bed. He had the most restful sleeps and did not wake until the sun was up in the morning. Then the angels would escort him back to the hospital. There he would remain all day, sleeping off and on, while his body healed. In between, he looked out of the window at the harbor. He enjoyed the gorgeous sunshine and stared at the beautiful boat that he knew he would venture onto at five o'clock. During his entire time in the coma, Ronnie did not experience any physical discomfort. The angels were around him every day, and they never left his room except when he did. Although dressed in civilian attire, they acted like security guards who had been especially trained to serve a royal family. They watched over Ronnie and made sure he was taken care of. They seemed to know what he needed and what he was thinking before he spoke a word. They made sure his every need was met, and that he was always comfortable.

Chapter 9

The Death Angel

One night, while Ronnie was in a coma and on the boat, the angels had a serious matter to discuss with him. They gathered around his bed and began speaking. "Ronnie," they said in a peaceful but earnest sort of way, "we want to ask you a question. Would you like to go away from here? Would you like to come with us? We will untie the boat and set sail for the far side of the ocean and go to better shores. Ronnie, there is no pain there, and you will never hurt again. We can go today. It is your choice. Would you like to come?"

Ronnie felt the peace and dignity that rested on the angels, and even though they were talking about his death, he trusted them completely. They were not traumatizing him. He thought of their words and the gracious invitation before him, and he knew that their offer was not out of place. He thought for just a brief moment and then responded. "My dear friends," he said ever-so-slowly, "I feel it is not time for me to go with you. My wife is waiting for me to return to the hospital. She is calling me, and I must go to be with her. For her sake, I should stay."

The angels simply nodded, as if they already knew what he would say but had to ask the question anyway. Quietly they left him to sleep without further ceremony or discussion. That was not the end, however, of Ronnie's invitation to depart from this life and go to a better place. A battle was being fought because of him, and for more than a month the balance of life tipped from one side to the other.

A day after the angels had asked the eternal question, Ronnie was in the hospital, sitting up in bed, at least in his mind. In reality, he was still in a coma. The reality he was experiencing was very different from the reality of those who were fighting to keep him alive. From our position, it is difficult to know if one reality is more real than the other. The scriptures are not silent on the matter. They say:

"Therefore we do not lose heart. Though outwardly we are wasting away, yet inwardly we are being renewed day by day. For our light and momentary troubles are achieving for us an eternal glory that far outweighs them all. So we fix our eyes not on what is seen, but on what is unseen. For what is seen is temporary, but what is unseen is eternal." 2 Cor. 4:16–18 NIV

An uneasy feeling suddenly came over Ronnie, and his gaze was decidedly drawn toward the corridor outside of his room. There, blocking the doorway, was a huge mountain of a man. His arms were folded across his chest, and his legs were comfortably spread like a soldier who had taken his position, standing at ease. He was a full seven-foot tall and wore a black, double-breasted Armani suit. Ronnie thought he looked like a well-groomed Italian. He had an olive-toned completion, was physically well-built, and would definitely fit in with nobility. He was a striking figure and not just of the aristocracy; he was more like a king. Confidence and boldness emanated from him and stuck to him on every side. Although he was not speaking, great skill and ancient wisdom seemed to be in him, and he carried an air as if he walked beneath a royal canopy and a red runner lay before his feet.

He was looking at Ronnie; in fact, he was staring, but not glaring with evil intent. Ronnie felt intimidated by the powerful giant, although the man was not trying to intimidate him. For all of his self-confidence and strength, he expressed a warm, personable feeling to Ronnie. He was the angel of death; a servant of the Most High God, and he was there on eternal business.

The death angel motioned to Ronnie to come to him. Then the three angels who were with Ronnie went and stood in front of the death angel. They blocked his pathway to Ronnie, but when the death angel began to step toward Ronnie, the three angels parted and let him pass. Ronnie did not move, and the angel began walking slowly toward his bed. Strange as it was, he brought peace, not terror, and Ronnie did not become frightened or anxious. Then the angel turned and stood by the wall and looked at Ronnie.

Ronnie remembers thinking that he was not to go with him. Without any words being spoken by the angel, Ronnie knew that he had come to take him to heaven. The two of them knew instinctively the thoughts of the other, and both of them were waiting for the outcome.

Ronnie was not ready to leave, but the angel began his forward motion toward Ronnie once again. Immediately the other angels came alongside of him and began talking with their taller, more powerful, fellow servant. Ronnie did not hear their words but knew they were convincing the death angel to wait on his decision and to leave Ronnie in his bed for now. Whatever they said was unknown to Ronnie, but after their conversation, the death angel paused and looked up at Ronnie. He gave a gentle nod, as if to say, "All right Ronnie, I will not take you this time." Then he turned and walked out of the room.

On one other occasion, Ronnie was visited by the death angel. The second time, Ronnie woke from sleep and found the angel standing in his room at the foot of his bed. The angel gave him such a start. The angel did not speak but stood still, looking at Ronnie. He was waiting, as if ready to hear a final word and begin his work. He started walking around the room. He continued waiting and listening but not saying a word, and every once in a while he stopped and looked at Ronnie and made a motion, as if he would come toward him. Then suddenly he would turn in a different direction. Ronnie wanted to hear him speak but knew instinctively that he could not talk with this angel as he had done with the other three.

He was not afraid of the messenger, and the death angel had most certainly not come to bring any trauma to Ronnie. He was there to minister on behalf of the Lord God Almighty. He was ready to carry Ronnie into the presence of God the Father and Jesus the Lamb, and he would have done it with gentle care and grace. Unseen forces were at work and time and again chose not to take Ronnie. The other three angels talked with the death angel a few times, and Ronnie noticed that they were shaking their heads. Ronnie's pathway had not been fully decided, and the angels, the Holy Spirit and the death angel were each doing their part to walk in harmony and perform the Father's will. The death angel was not detained because of the wonderful work of the doctors and nurses. It was the prayers of the saints that delayed his actions and stayed his hand. Prayers were filling the throne room of heaven, and God was moved by those prayers and instructed the angels accordingly. Those prayers reversed the decision of the Almighty over Ronnie's life.

The death angel remained in Ronnie's room for most of the day and then as suddenly and as abruptly as he had come, he was gone. Ronnie wondered what had happened to alter his decision.

There are two types of spiritual beings that converge at the site of one's death. They are demonic spirits of death under the commands of the devil and death angels who are sent as ambassadors of heaven. They latter serve the Lord.

Demon spirits are like vultures that prey upon the dead. They prey upon those near death and those who deserve death. They are a foul and an evil company whose commission is to steal, kill, and destroy people. They are enemies of God, but they cannot hurt him personally, so they hurt people who are made in his image. Demons are arrogant and are at war with God, yet they are insanely jealous of the invitation and privilege that mankind has with him. They aim to bring sickness and premature death to people. When the time of death comes, they will do all they can to make that death a time of torment and terror. They will even try to pervert the proper and godly death of a saint. That is why death is called our last enemy. God designed people for friendship and fellowship with him. Humankind is destined to inherit God's eternal and universal bounty and to rule the earth alongside of Jesus. People have the gift of God's Spirit and access to heaven, and while demons have superior powers, they are put under man's feet. They hate this and do all they can to hinder our personal well-being and obstruct God's purpose with humanity. Our goal is to resist them, cast them out, and agree with heaven for their failure. Fighting the spirits of death is a monumental battle, but greater is he who is with us than he who is in the world. In other words, our God is bigger than theirs.

The other spiritual being who comes to the site of death is a death angel. He is a servant of the Almighty and gathers those who have died to take them to their eternal dwelling place. These angels are extremely powerful and execute the will of God perfectly. They will take the vile and the pure, the sinner and the saint, and only the Holy Spirit can stop or delay them. They may cause death as a judgment of God, as it was with the firstborn of Egypt in the time of the Exodus. They also bring death to the children of God, but that is no judgment; it is a victory. They will protect a soul from the vultures and take one's life from the earth in an honorable and glorious fashion. They take great care with this transition. They will end a believer's life with dignity. After death, they have the honor of carrying God's people into his presence. They realize that these are the redeemed,

God's precious possession. People who walk with God are the long-awaited harvest that was paid for at the cross. An angel will never carry anything more important than a saint. How delicate and caring he is with this cargo, and how highly honored he is to serve the Ancient of Days and Jesus the Lamb in this way.

Chapter 10

Marathon Runners

As far as Ronnie's medical condition was concerned, a few things were progressing well but not quickly, and he was still threatened by death. His abdomen was now sewn together, but by all accounts, he was in critical condition. On the fifteenth day of his coma, the doctors agreed that other urgent matters needed attention. Dr. Sutton, the orthopedic surgeon, proceeded with plans to do preliminary work on Ronnie's leg. It had been twenty-one days since Ronnie's accident, and no work had been done on his shattered leg or pelvis because of his life-threatening, abdominal trauma. Without moving Ronnie from his bed, Dr. Sutton drilled three holes through his left leg and set three pegs in place so mild traction could be applied to keep Ronnie's leg from any additional fusing of the bones in wrong places. Metal bars protruded above the knee, below the knee, and through his ankle. They stuck out about four inches on either side. No bone was set, and no corrective surgery was performed at this time, but the doctor was able to take some safeguards in preparation for future leg and pelvic operations. Until now Ronnie's legs had not been a priority. Still, they were a mess. If he somehow survived his battle for life, it was certain that he would never be able to use his legs for running or strenuous activity.

The hospital's life-support systems were keeping Ronnie alive for the moment, but the battle for his survival was a long way from over. Soon his temperature rose again to critical levels. His blood pressure dropped drastically, and major arteries in his body were collapsing. Ronnie's nurse informed Clarice of the on-going changes in his situation. She reported every serious detail regarding his condition. Ronnie's body had gone through so much and was once again failing to respond to the life-sustaining treatments. Ronnie relapsed into massive organ failure, and once more everything shut down. Another desperate crisis lay before the medical team.

Medical professionals are often called upon to go the extra mile and endure immense pressures. They give of themselves when they seem to have nothing more to give. Many times they must stay on the job and apply themselves long after their energy has been spent. They may desperately want to leave and go home, but they cannot, because they are compelled to stick with the emergency at hand and do all they can to see it pass. The entire season of working with Ronnie was such a time as that for the medical staff. This was a marathon race, and they were challenged to the limit, but they pressed forward and continued to care and give of their very best for Ronnie, right to the end.

This segment of the battle lasted for days, and Ronnie's life was in flux. Waves of trouble seemed to attend him constantly, like those that crash relentlessly on the shore. His health went up and down, back and forth, in sustained rhythms like the tides of the ocean. He would appear to be stable for a few hours, and then the bottom would drop out. The doctors would once again work under great duress to bring him through the emergency until he was stable again.

Prayers were lifted around the clock. The large network of Christians praying for Ronnie continued to grow. Major denominations and Christian TV networks were soliciting prayers for Ronnie. Other churches in the community besides East Side called upon their parishioners to pray for Ronnie. Clarice and her local church family were increasing in faith, fasting, and prayer, and they simply would not let go or let up. They continued their extensive prayer vigil day after day and night after night. In addition to the private prayer assignments that they loaded upon themselves, they met in groups to pray. They prayed at the church, in homes, at restaurants, in the hospital waiting room, and even in the parking lot. Sometimes they found a no-doubt zone, and their prayers broke through enemy lines and connected with heaven. Other times the intercessors felt as though they were stuck in the battle trenches, and they could not move or make any spiritual headway at all. Still they continued. They often quoted the scripture:

"If my people, who are called by my name, will humble themselves and pray and seek my face and turn from their wicked ways, then will I hear from heaven and will forgive their sin and will heal their land." 2 Chron. 7:14 NIV

Although the scripture was first given to the Israelites and applied to prayer in their newly built temple, those praying for Ronnie took hold of it for themselves. They believed if their prayers met God's conditions, he would do something positive for them just as he did for Israel. He would release healing.

Clarice's will to fight for Ronnie did not subside. Rather than mellow out as the days passed, Clarice grew more vigilant. Her desperate, heartfelt cries to God for Ronnie's healing did not waiver. She knew that the Holy Spirit alone could sustain and strengthen her for the intense battle she was in, and she persevered.

One day she walked into intensive care and was caught in the path of a spiritual hurricane. The doctors were rushing around Ronnie and yelling at each other as though they needed to hear each other over the noise and commotion of a violent storm. They were trying to hold on to him and sustain him against what seemed to be impossible odds. Clarice sensed the gravity of the situation. The air was filled with desperate cries, the atmosphere was charged with panic, and the seriousness of the situation grabbed Clarice's heart and squeezed. Pain shot through her body and, in an instant without a second thought, she dropped to her knees right in front of the nurses' station and cried out to God as loud as she could. "Oh God, please come," she screamed. "In Jesus name, have mercy on Ronnie. Come and heal him. We need your help, right now. Oh God, help the doctors. Oh God, let your power come on them and let your power come on Ronnie. Keep him alive. Sustain him, Lord. Oh God, rescue us in this moment, give life back to Ronnie."

Before Ronnie's accident, Clarice was always conscious of what people thought of her. She never wanted to stand out or draw attention to herself. She was somewhat shy, but now all of that had been shaken off. She carried on emphatically, voicing her prayers to heaven right in front of the medical staff, the patients, and the other visitors in ICU. No one stopped her or tried to move her. Those with authority were busy working on Ronnie, and any timid person would surely keep their distance from Clarice when she was in warrior mode. At that moment, Clarice did not give any thought to what others might think or do; she only cared what God might do. Protocol did not matter to her when her husband's life was on the line.

The doctors had never seen anything like it. Many people come into the hospital and pray for the sick, but Clarice was much more aggressive. This was not just a lunatic lady caught in a fit of emotion. The doctors saw through that possible misinterpretation. She was a woman of faith, a spiritual fighter who believed that God would answer her desperate prayers. Like the woman in the Bible who broke through the crowd to touch the hem of Christ's garment, she was reaching out to the God who performs miracles. The doctors were doing all they could, but they needed a miracle. Under normal conditions, Clarice would never have obtained permission to do the things she did. Perhaps some did not appreciate her exuberance. The ones who did may have believed that her ability to get away with everything was a miracle in itself—a smaller, secondary miracle to Ronnie's healing, but nevertheless a miracle.

So Clarice prayed and, once again God stayed the hand of death. He extended his grace, and Ronnie pulled through. The doctor's hands had become an extension of God's hands, and they knew that a power beyond their own was at work in Ronnie to bring him back from the dead so many times.

The work with Ronnie had become crisis management. The doctors worked diligently to systematically deal with the many issues at hand. They endeavored to wean Ronnie from the ventilator, which he had been on for weeks. They removed it, and he began breathing on his own. A doctor friend was visiting the hospital, and he met with Clarice. "How is Ronnie doing?" he asked.

"Oh, just fine. We are so glad. He's just come off the ventilator. He's doing just great," Clarice replied.

After the doctor friend saw Ronnie, he was extremely concerned. Sweat was pouring out of Ronnie and running down his face. His body was dripping wet. "Clarice," he said, "you need to get Ronnie back on that ventilator immediately. It is so difficult for him to breathe right now; he will not survive. He is working much too hard. He is still in a coma, but he is literally fighting for his life. Right now he is like a marathon runner, struggling to find and pull in his next breath. He is gasping for air. At this rate his lungs are going to collapse, and his heart will stop. Clarice, please ask the doctor to get that ventilator back in place."

The doctors agreed, and over the next few days they took the ventilator off and put it back on again several times. Ronnie continued to struggle, and eventually the doctors told Clarice they would have to give him a tracheotomy because his breathing was so labored. They said they could only wait for another twelve hours. Then they must cut open his neck and bronchia and perform the tracheotomy.

Clarice prayed as she had done many times before. By the time the twelve hours had passed, Ronnie's breathing had improved so much that the tracheotomy was not necessary. The ventilator was off, and this time it stayed off.

Clarice sat on a chair at Ronnie's side, her body half leaning against the mattress and bedding. Her hand was gently resting on his. He was lifeless, and her mind wandered as she looked beyond the hospital window. She was fascinated with the deep color of the azure-blue sky and the patterns in the clouds that gave the impression that two people had stretched them out and pulled them tight like massive sheets of silk. It looked like the sea was in the sky. Then she noticed distant hazy mountains, far off at the back of the scene. Tropical islands rose out of the water in front of them, as if a painter had put them there to add distance and depth to his painting. She studied the panoramic picture and thought how beautiful it was. It will soon move on and disappear. No one will ever see the amazing vista that I have just seen.

She was daydreaming, looking beyond the stainless steel, intravenous stand at the end of the bed, past the TV monitors, and out the window to the world of wonder. She was paying no attention to anything in the room. Then she started thinking about her house. What condition would it be in, and what of the store and Ronnie's restaurant? Their key employees had come to the hospital in the early days and had convinced her that everything would be taken care of. She did not doubt their efforts to help or their good intentions, and for thirty days she hardly gave the outside world any thought. Now she wondered what mess might she find when she finally got out of here. What things might have suffered without her or Ronnie there to give their usual oversight? No one quite cares for things the way you do, she thought. She turned her head and looked at Ronnie and a shock hit her—full-force.

Ronnie was looking right back at her. His eyes were half open and moving slowly, as if to study her face. Instantly she leaped to her feet and turned toward Ronnie, still holding his hand. "Are you there, honey?" she questioned softly. "Are you there?"

He did not even attempt to speak. He made no sound and was perfectly motionless, except for his eyes. Clarice leaned in again. This time she squeezed his hand and rubbed it tenderly with her own. "I love you, dear. I really, really love you, honey. Can you hear me?"

Clarice looked toward the hall, through the open door to the nurses' station. She didn't see a soul. "Nurse, nurse, is anyone out there?" she yelled as loud as she could.

"Nuuurse, nurse, nurse, nur ..." Before she could finish, a white-gowned nurse came running around the corner and entered the room.

Ronnie had come out of the coma.

Chapter 11

Brain Damage

Several nurses crowded around Ronnie, checking his vital signs and trying to draw a cognitive response from him. Although they were trained for intensive care, seeing a patient come out of an extended coma was not an everyday occurrence. The head nurse had taken charge. She was efficient and deliberate. Her many years of working with trauma patients had given her a great portfolio of expertise. She was a natural leader. Her subordinates loved and respected her. Immediately and instinctively she followed the step-by-step procedure for coma recovery. She was calm, and although there was a noted excitement buzzing in the air, the nurse had her wits about her. She was methodically doing exactly as her instructors and experience had taught her. She gave clear directions to the other nurses. They followed her example with calm resolve, each doing their respective tasks. The head nurse was holding Ronnie's hand and wiping his face. She was looking into his eyes as if to see inside his being to find his soul. She began asking questions of Ronnie, the same series of questions over and over again. She was patient and gentle, but forthright and persistent.

Clarice had backed away and was standing by the door to Ronnie's room. She was so excited that her heart was charging like a racehorse. She did not know what to expect. What was supposed to happen? How should Ronnie be acting? She only knew that his eyes were wide open, and the nurses had stepped forward to work with him. They seemed to be doing their job well, but Clarice wondered if they were supposed to do something else to help Ronnie recover. Was it proper procedure to stimulate Ronnie? Should they be giving him some intravenous drug like adrenalin to act as a catalyst? Could they, at this stage, do something too quickly or too slowly? Maybe this was simply an act of God like having a baby—you wait, and when the time is right, labor begins, pain comes, and very naturally the child is born. Is that what was happening here? Do we just stand back and let the natural, God-given recovery unfold?

She had a myriad of questions running through her head. No one had talked to Clarice about post-coma recovery. She did not know what might happen, or what she should expect. They had been so focused on just keeping him from death that they failed to talk about the possible stages of restoration. She stood and watched all that the nurses were doing, while under her breath she talked to God, thanking and asking and thanking him again.

There was nothing else she could do, or was there? Suddenly Clarice went into her task-oriented mode. This had become her regular pattern. It was her place to be spiritually responsible, so she rushed to the waiting room to find help. She went to solicit prayer support from her friends. A couple of visitors had just arrived, and she shared the change in Ronnie's condition with them. She did not linger, however. Her thoughts became clearer. She walked swiftly to the pay phone to call her faithful prayer recruiter, Sandy. As usual, it was a morale booster to both parties when these ladies talked. Once again, Sandy rose to the occasion. She made calls to inform the prayer network. The news was fabulous. People were elated and freshly inspired to pray with renewed fervor when they heard that Ronnie was out of the coma.

One of Ronnie's doctors, a neurologist, arrived in his room, and after hearing the details from the head nurse, continued to investigate Ronnie's condition. It had been more than forty-five minutes since Ronnie's eyes had opened, and still no other cognitive responses were coming from him. The doctor did not know, but Ronnie reported later that he could hear his words. They were garbled and faint and seemed far off, as if the doctor were speaking in the other room. He did, however, recognize some of those words. He heard, "He has brain damage." That is all Ronnie remembered, because immediately after hearing the doctor's diagnosis, he slipped back into a coma. He fell into remission, and once more departed from the conscious world of man.

Clarice did not know whether this relapse was normal. Did the doctors expect some going back and forth at the beginning of one's recovery? Regardless, she remained steady in her faith, and her newfound hope did not waiver. Ronnie was on his way back, and she would make no room for doubt. In a couple of hours he returned to consciousness, and this time he stayed there.

The doctor continued his work with Ronnie and found his neural responses extremely slow and mostly non-responsive. He told Clarice not to expect too much. This put in motion another episode of anxiety for Clarice, because the doctor's report included the strong likelihood of brain damage. Clarice feared that possibility. The thought of it had lodged in the back of her mind since its first mention, a month earlier. The nurse said very little, but gave Clarice some basic instructions. She was to sit with Ronnie, letting him have lots of rest and sleep. When he was awake, she was to talk and communicate with him as much as possible.

Ronnie did come around, and this time more than his eyes were moving. He moved his hand when Clarice rubbed it, and he turned his head to look at her when she spoke to him. Ronnie seemed to recognize her, but he did not speak. His facial expressions communicated that he was not comfortable. He acted agitated and restless. Perhaps he was in pain, Clarice thought. With each passing minute, his emotions intensified, and his awareness of the room around him and his own awful condition sharpened. Suddenly, to everyone's surprise, Ronnie began to speak. But no, it was not speech; it was sounds. He groaned and moaned and uttered combinations of unrecognizable syllables. "It's okay, dear," Clarice, whispered, "I can't understand you, honey. You keep trying. It will come. Be patient, dear."

Ronnie was neither patient nor calm. He was visibly frustrated and cranky, like a small child awakened from a deep sleep before his sleep was finished. He was trying to tell Clarice something, but the words would not come out. It seemed that his mouth had forgotten the skill of speech and the remembrance of human language. Try as he did, Ronnie could not communicate clearly. He became frustrated, and frustration led to anguish, and anguish turned to anger. It was a frozen anger that was rapidly thawing out. Ronnie's noises were faint and sporadic, and they sounded horrible. It was pathetic, and Clarice felt helpless, because whatever she said or did to comfort or reason with Ronnie resulted in nothing. Her words were immediately lost, like mist dissipating in air. She tried and tried, but with every effort she grew more frustrated. The emotions that welled within her began to rattle her, and she could not hold back the tears gathering in her eyes. The nurse watching from her station in the hall came to rescue Clarice. "Don't worry, darlin'," she said comfortingly. "Give it time, honey. It'll be okay. Ronnie will be just fine."

Clarice did not want to leave Ronnie, but she was distraught, and since the nurse had relieved her, she left the room for a much-needed break. She had to catch her breath and hear from God. Once again the hospital chapel proved to be an invaluable place of refuge and resolve. She sat there alone, talking with God about the phrase brain damage. She would not receive it. She spoke against it and prayed that it would not be so. Finally her prayers turned to thanksgiving, and she repeatedly uttered nothing but "Thank you Jesus," over and over again. In a final, soothing whisper, she said, "Thank you Jesus."

Peace came back and a quiet tempo returned to her soul. She stayed in the chapel for a long time, soaking in the manifest presence of God's Holy Spirit. She did not want to leave. She felt the presence of the Lord caressing her and containing her. She felt as though she had come together again. She thought this is just what the doctor—Dr. Jesus—has ordered for me, and it is good medicine indeed.

Much later in the day, after gathering her composure and regaining her sense of direction, she met with friends. She ate a meal, received prayer, and felt much encouraged. When Clarice returned to Ronnie's room, she found him fast asleep. This time, however, she was better prepared to communicate with her mate. She brought with her a pen and a pad of paper. Maybe Ronnie's vocal cords were not ready to speak. Perhaps he could write his thoughts, communicating with her using pen and paper.

It was the following day before Ronnie woke. His first day out of coma was very tiring. When he slept, it was long and deep. Clarice was eager to see what progress had been gained in the night. She was enthusiastic about her idea of communicating with pen and paper. He did seem better. The nurse had spoon-fed Ronnie his first bite of food, a tiny portion of Jello pudding. Beyond that, there was little improvement in Ronnie's condition. When Clarice began talking with him, he responded in the same way as he had the day before. He was unable to speak a single word that made sense. The sounds that came were slow and slurred. But Ronnie tried, and the more he did, the tenser and more anxious he became. Nevertheless, Clarice was determined that Ronnie's behavior was not going to upset her like it had the day before. She calmed him. The nurse had raised his bed on a slight incline to feed him, so she thought it a perfect opportunity to try to communicate with him using pen and paper.

Clarice slowly and carefully asked Ronnie to write his thoughts on paper. Whatever he was trying to say, if he could just write it down, she would be able to help him. Clarice steadied the writing pad that was fastened securely to a clipboard, and she placed the pen in Ronnie's hand. Without looking at her, Ronnie knew exactly what to do. He could not lift his arm, but Clarice placed it on the board. Although it was not easy, he held the pen, and to Clarice's joy, he began to write. At first the pen moved very slowly and slid off the page and dropped onto the floor, but it was a start. He tried again. This time he was able to write, but all that came to the page was a slow scribble.

Clarice worked with him patiently for close to an hour, waiting and then trying again, but the doodle remained unrecognizable. It was just scribble, and Ronnie was tiring. He wrote irregular, elongated, crooked circles. The doodle looked liked the work of a two-year-old. Ronnie had no energy or strength, so he could barely do what he did. He was not fast like a child might be. That was all he was able to do. He became increasingly frustrated and began groaning like a wounded beast. Ronnie was so weak, but that would improve. Clarice was now more concerned with his inner man. She wondered how much pain and anguish was stirring in his heart.

As if there were a carefully timed evil conspiracy, the neurologist came into the room at that moment to check on Ronnie. He saw what Clarice was attempting to do and looked at the pages in the writing pad bearing Ronnie's weak scribble. He tried to talk with Ronnie, but nothing had changed. Ronnie's only response was slow, garbled noises that had no resemblance to human speech. No matter how hard the doctor tried, Ronnie could not communicate with him in any sensible way—not by talking or writing or even through hand gestures. All that came from Ronnie was a look of desperation. It communicated aggravation and anger. All of this confirmed the doctor's diagnosis. "Mrs. Holden," he said, "I am sorry, but now I have no doubt.

Your husband has severe brain damage, and it is likely that he may not improve much from the way he is right now."

Clarice had been resisting the thought of brain damage. She held to her position, refusing to believe that the doctor's words were true. Why would God answer so many prayers and sustain Ronnie's life so that he would be mentally handicapped for the rest of his life? She fought the idea; she prayed against it. She called upon the church to engage in spiritual warfare against what she deemed to be a demonic lie, the most recent attack from the devil. The prayer meetings went into full gear once again. Some of the church members met with Clarice for an extended evening of intercession and supplication in the hospital. That night, when Clarice laid her head down on the waiting room sofa, she wept and wept. She prayed and wept until she cried herself to sleep.

The next morning, Ronnie was still unable to communicate, but something was worse. His spirit had retreated, and his heart had grown cold. When Clarice attempted to speak with him, he made no effort to respond. At least before he was groaning or trying to scribble, but no more. Ronnie had gone quiet. Several times Clarice attempted to draw out some response from her husband but to no avail. He simply would not respond. Finally Clarice exploded.

Whether it was good strategy or simple frustration, it is hard to say, but she began to yell at Ronnie. "Ronnie," she said, glaring at her husband, "I have been fighting for your life for a month, and others in the church and from all over this country have come to visit you and have spent time praying for you. They have fought for your survival and your recovery, and now it is time for you to fight as well." She was marching around his bed and waiving her hands in the air. "Ronnie," she continued, louder than ever, "you had better do something and you better start doing it now. You need to fight for your life. This is no time to give up, Ronnie. I want you to fight. Fight! There is some fighting, Ronnie, that only you can do. Come on, Ronnie! Fight with us—fight for your life!"

Clarice had no idea that Ronnie was beginning to think more clearly and was becoming more and more aware of his situation. He was in turmoil, discomfort, and a great deal of pain. Anxiety had overtaken him, and his condition was nearly unbearable. He still had the medical halo. Many of the tubes and wires were still attached to him. His leg was in a brace, being supported and pulled toward some metal frame at the end of his bed. He could hardly move, and when he tried to, it was awful. His body and mind just would not function. Besides all of this, Ronnie was now vomiting whatever juices and bits of food he had in his stomach. He was unable to move his body, so whatever he vomited came out onto the front of his hospital gown. He was an awful mess, and he felt as though he were trapped and dying in a useless body. Ronnie was delirious and delusional. All he remembered was his time on the boat with the angels. He felt so sick and so awful that he just wanted to die. He had changed his mind about going with angels. Now, more than anything else, he wanted to go away with them. He could not bear his condition. He had come from a place of perfect peace while he was in the coma out into a place of anguish, confusion, and turmoil. It was more than he could handle. He desperately wanted to go with the angels to the place where he would not feel any of this anymore. In his mind he called for the angels to return.

The next morning, Dr. Maxwell wanted to talk with Clarice. He had the written report from the night nurse. It said there was an outburst from Clarice. "Mrs. Holden," he said, "I understand that last night there was a ruckus in here between you and Mr. Holden."

"Ruckus, oh no," responded Clarice, "everything was just fine doctor. No, there was no ruckus here."

Doctor Maxwell let it slide and said no more about the matter. Then to everyone's surprise, while the doctor was still talking, Ronnie began to speak. At first it was mumbles and slow broken syllables, but he was definitely speaking English. Hallelujah! This was like Christmas for Clarice. She was so excited, so thrilled, she could hardly contain herself. Her pent-up emotions of grief and frustration vanished, and her heart flooded with joy. When she told her church friends in the waiting room, there was a burst of celebration and excitement that sounded like the best of parties in full swing. It was one more miraculous breakthrough, and the news spread far and wide through the prayer network: Ronnie was talking.

By the end of the day, Ronnie was speaking enough that if one paid careful attention, one could understand his words. Ronnie tried with all he had to get his thoughts across to Clarice and Sandy. What he communicated, however, was not the joyful response of the intercessors. Rather, he shared his pain, terror, and hopelessness. He wanted to die. There were no words of wanting to stay or to be with Clarice or his family or friends. He did not seem glad to see them. He just wanted to get away and leave his unbearable situation behind.

Clarice didn't take any of this personally. However, when Ronnie started to talk in slow broken phrases about seeing and visiting angels and going on the boat with them every day at five o'clock, she could not stand it. His words were garbled, and the message came out like the slurs of a drunken man. This, she thought, was brain damage. This is insanity, hallucinations, hearing voices, and seeing things that did not actually happen. People in a coma do not remember things. "Oh no," she said, "We will have none of that. None of that is real Ronnie, and we renounce it right now. You stop talking about that. We will have no mental illness and no brain failure here. I do not want you to be labeled brain-damaged. Do not talk about that boat."

Ronnie did not understand. He challenged Clarice's advice. Clarice tried to explain. She would not budge on her assessment or change her counsel to Ronnie. He became extremely tired but stuck to his story. He would not renounce or deny a single, frail word.

Clarice was angry. If there is any truth in this, she thought, then Ronnie has had a great time while I have been fighting the hosts of hell. He has been enjoying himself, free from pain and despair for twenty-one days, while I have carried his struggle, challenged demons, fought with doctors, wrestled with God, and almost come to the end of myself over worry and grief. I have not left this hospital for thirty days. I have slept on a hard sofa in a public waiting room, while he has been with angels. I can't believe it is true. She knew, however, that this was no time to argue with Ronnie, and so she let it go. He was in no condition for conflict, and she was glad to have him back, no matter what state he was in. Soon he fell into a deep sleep once again.

When Clarice and Sandy rejoined Ronnie in the morning, he was in a panic. He was still unable to move, but he was frantic. His emotions were in a dreadful state. He was screaming, even though his speech was disconnected and slurred. It took quite a while for him to calm down and tell them what had happened.

The three angels had visited him again, but this visit was not at all like the others. This encounter was frightful and terrifying. To this day, Ronnie is not sure why he was allowed to see what he saw. The angels came into his room and seemed desperate. They were not alone. Walking with them was a young lady, perhaps only sixteen years of age. She had washed-out, red hair, and her skin was grayish blue. Although she was walking, she was limp and lifeless. She was dead, and the angels were waiting for the death angel to come.

Before hearing any explanation, Ronnie knew that a dark and evil thing had happened to the girl. Immediately he was inundated with the feelings of her trauma. The angels stayed for a long time, and Ronnie began questioning them. "What happened here? Where is she going? What are you doing with her?" he asked.

The angels did not speak, but suddenly the girl spoke: "I committed suicide. They're taking me somewhere. I don't know where they are taking me."

Ronnie was terrified, as if he had just been exposed to an awful horror movie and wished that he hadn't seen it. Feelings of anxiety and panic rushed in. This was not a timely death. This girl should not have died. This should not have happened. She should still be alive. It was absolutely awful. A thief had robbed her and taken her life. She did not have the time or opportunity to fulfill her destiny. Ronnie was grieved and upset. He was beside himself. Finally the angels and the girl left, but the vision remained a fixture in Ronnie's mind.

Later, Ronnie thought about it often. He felt that this might have been a prophetic warning and had not actually happened yet. It was about the future. Perhaps her untimely death could be stopped if someone could get to her and help her. Perhaps the angels saw the fervent prayers of Clarice and her friends and wanted them to pray for the girl.

Maybe the angels wanted Ronnie to know that not everyone experiences the kind of care he experienced when trouble comes. He wondered if the angels had brought the girl to show him that even though he was in an awful state, there are many in the world much worse off. Ronnie gained insight concerning the battle over the lives of people, and he gained much more compassion for those less fortunate than himself.

It was not certain where the girl's eternal home would be, but it was clear she did not fulfill her destiny on earth. It was indeed sad if the girl died without repenting of her sins and receiving Jesus Christ as her personal savior.

The girl's story was reminiscent of the Egyptians who failed to apply the lamb's blood on their doorposts during the time of the Exodus. The lamb's blood represented the blood of Jesus

Christ in prophetic foreshadowing. The death angel came and took every firstborn child who was not under the blood. To this day, that time is called the Passover. For those who obeyed the Lord, the death angel passed over, and no one was harmed (Exodus, chapters 11–12). The blood of Jesus protects those who believe that Jesus died to save us from our sins and who confess that he is our Savior. Then we are saved into eternal life in the presence of the Lord.

Ronnie was left with a stark memory of the dead girl. Her appearance served as a serious warning to examine his own life and make sure that he was right with God. He also was reminded to look beyond his private life to the salvation of others. Regardless of his personal trauma, God was continuing to ask Ronnie to lead others to him.

Ronnie communicated the urgency of the matter with Clarice. She and Sandy prayed with Ronnie for the girl's life and for her salvation.

There was another purpose that came from this traumatic visit. Ronnie realized that he must fight for life and destiny, even if it was his own. Soon after, Ronnie had new strength in his soul. He began to fight for his own survival and well-being.

Chapter 12

The Shadow of the Almighty

By now, Ronnie had become something of a poster boy around the hospital. When people talked about him at a patient's bedside, in the back rooms, or in the halls, he was affectionately known as "Miracle Boy." His story became a platform of encouragement for every preacher and well-wisher who was endeavoring to encourage a sick friend or relative at the hospital.

Every day Ronnie improved, but it was often unnoticeable. His progress was extremely slow. Medically speaking, the next major task was to operate on his left leg. Although his pelvis was broken, it was healing without help from the doctors. Ronnie had been immobile for the entire time he was in the coma, and the fractures in his pelvis had begun to fuse together and mend on their own. His liver, kidneys, and spleen healed as well, but his leg was another matter.

Dr. Sutton had been unable to operate on Ronnie's leg for an entire month since the accident. Now it was at the top of the priority list. It was a massive operation. They removed all of the pieces of crushed and splintered bone from Ronnie's leg and knee. Then they delicately wrapped flesh, veins, cartilage, and nerves around a man-made metal skeleton. It was a lengthy task involving tremendous skill and expertise. Dr. Sutton inserted a titanium rod into Ronnie's leg. It started at his hip and extended to his ankle. The rod had a titanium swivel joint at the knee and was joined with ball in socket at the hip and screws at the ankle. The operation was a marvel of modern science, but it would take more than a year before Ronnie would be able to walk without help.

After forty days, Ronnie's recovery was so good that they moved him to the hospital's rehabilitation center. Good recovery is a relative term, however, because Ronnie was still very weak. He could not roll on his side or lift his arm without help. He still had a colostomy bag. He continued with an intravenous drip and was continually exhausted. His ability to see was so poor that he was unable to read a word, even with glasses. His speech remained slurred and slow, and he was in a lot of pain. Still, progress is progress. Everyone who knew what he had been through was encouraged. The doctors ruled out the possibility of brain damage, which was a great relief to Clarice.

Upon his arrival at rehab, Ronnie requested the removal of his morphine drip. Even though he was in pain, he remembered his battle with drugs in 84 and did not want even a remote possibility of a relapse with that demon of addiction. They gave him Tylenol instead, and during his entire time at rehab Ronnie never complained about his condition. That does not mean that things were not difficult. He depended heavily on Clarice.

It was against policy for any relative or friend to stay overnight at the rehab center. Furthermore, daytime visits were limited. Against her will, Clarice was forced to go home. She stayed at her cousin's home in Wilmington, visiting Ronnie as often as the staff allowed.

The rehab workers spoon-fed Ronnie for the first day, but he was so sick that he could hardly keep anything down. On the second day, something went wrong. The hospital was understaffed, and an oversight was made. A new worker brought him breakfast. She placed his food on a tray beside his bed and left.

She was covering more responsibilities than was normal and did not know Ronnie or his condition. The food remained there all morning, and Ronnie could neither roll toward it nor lift his arm to get it. He was an invalid. He still had the halo on his head because of his broken neck. His arm muscles were atrophied from the coma. His stomach muscles were dysfunctional because of the incision to his abdomen that the doctors had been unable to close for twelve days. Without stomach muscles it was impossible to sit up. As if that were not enough, his smashed leg had now been sliced from top to bottom and sewn back together. It lay on the bed like a limp rag. So many parts of his body were in need of healing and rehabilitation that Ronnie Holden was incapable of doing anything for himself.

When Clarice came to visit Ronnie, she found him frightened, upset, and emotionally exhausted. No one had been there for him, and he was in no condition to be left alone for so long. He was crying when Clarice arrived, and through his tears he begged her not to leave him again. After that fiasco, the rehab center broke the rules and permitted Clarice to stay at the hospital to care for Ronnie. Like before, Clarice found a place to sleep in the waiting room. Unfortunately there was no sofa. For the next ten nights she slept on a wood-framed, leatherette lounge chair. It proved to be a most uncomfortable bed, but she was glad to be back with Ronnie, and he was thrilled to have her.

Clarice was all Ronnie needed. From that moment on he had a pleasant, joyful disposition, and people loved working with him. Everyone who visited him enjoyed his fellowship, and they did not want to leave. Drew and Rebecca were the two physiotherapists who worked regularly with Ronnie, and they were fabulous. They became good friends with Ronnie and Clarice and later visited them at their home to share an evening meal. They liked their work. Although rehabilitating Ronnie was a massive task, they felt privileged to play a part in his recovery.

They were great encouragers and patient workers. They would roll him out of bed and take him to the workout room, propped in a wheelchair. Whether in bed or in the wheelchair, Ronnie had to be surrounded with pillows to sit up. He could not stand at all. The physiotherapists began to work on his upper body. Even that was extremely basic. For days they lifted his arms for him and bent and moved his legs, because he was incapable of any self-generated movement.

After twelve days of physiotherapy Ronnie stood with the help of the workers. Still he could not put any weight on his left leg. He could only remain standing for ten seconds before the team had to lift him back into his wheelchair. They also worked on his hand and eye coordination. With the help of pulleys and cables, muscle was built up, and strength slowly returned to Ronnie's arms.

While at the rehab center, Ronnie was visited by the hospital psychiatrist. He asked Ronnie how he was doing and what he thought of all that had happened to him. Ronnie's reply was amazing. He said, "Doctor, I am so thankful just to be alive. I give God the credit for that. I am not mad at anyone—not the driver who hit me or anyone else. I am coming out of this, and I will be totally healed one day. The accident that I had was just a pothole on the highway of life, and I have passed by it, and I am on my way to recovery. Doctor, I am a blessed man."

His outlook on life was so positive that the psychiatrist never returned. Then Ronnie decided to call his mother. Someone else had to hold the phone for him. He could not talk for long, because it made him tired, but it was great to speak with her. Ronnie's brother had given Mom the mild version of Ronnie's story, so she was prepared for the call. She asked him how he was doing, and Ronnie replied, "I'm doing just wonderful, Mom." And he meant every word of it.

Ronnie's behavior was such a powerful testimony to workers and visitors. They were constantly asking him questions about his accident and recovery. They believed they had an unusual opportunity to talk with someone who had stared death in the face and survived. People are naturally inquisitive about death, trauma, miracles, and the supernatural. They wanted to know if there were some secret behind Ronnie's story. What they heard Ronnie say and what they saw when they looked at him were inspiring, and all who talked with him were drawn closer to the Lord. The answers that Ronnie gave regarding his recovery always pointed to the goodness of God. He said that God was his secret. He was gracious and mentioned the doctors, the hospital staff, and his friends. He never failed to give special tribute to Clarice, but after saying all of that, he gave testimony to the love of God. He made sure that God received the ultimate praise and glory for the resurrection of his life.

For Ronnie, it was all about God. God at work in the doctors, God at work though the prayers of Clarice and her friends, and God at work through angels. The Holy Spirit was with him, directly watching over him, protecting him, and healing him. Ronnie knew that his life and all he had were gifts from God. He spent his private moments talking with the Lord and thanking him for his goodness and grace. Ronnie had a lot of time on his hands, and he carefully reviewed all he had gone through since the accident. He played everything back in his mind like studying the frames of a movie. He could hardly believe the details but knew they were true. God had released miracles on every part of the journey. Ronnie acquired a new love for the scriptures, because he wanted to draw as close to God as possible. God often speaks to people through the Bible, but Ronnie was unable to read for himself. For some reason his eyes would not focus on the printed page for almost a year. His vision was very blurred. When someone offered to read a portion of scripture to him, it was a treat.

Ronnie felt the presence of the Holy Spirit living in him and watching over him. Whatever demons had troubled or attacked him at one stage or another during the battle were gone. They had lost the fight and had given up and moved on. It happened to Jesus, who was tempted and tried by the devil for forty days and nights in the wilderness. After losing that battle against the Son of God, the scriptures reveal that Satan left him for a season, and the angels came and ministered comfort to Jesus (Matthew 4:1–11).

Ronnie was in a similar place. The devil had left him. The peace of God had come. Although he no longer saw angels, he knew that the Holy Spirit was present. The Lord ministered to him and comforted him continually. Ronnie knew he was under the shadow of the Almighty, and he reveled in the goodness and kindness of his Heavenly Father.

Clarice was extremely thankful as well, but she went from one battleground to another. The immediate crisis for Ronnie's life had lifted, and her strength seemed to flat-line, as if someone had pulled the plug. She felt that her energy was gone now that the emergency was over. She, however, could not reduce her responsibilities, and that was difficult. She was trying to brace herself for a new battle—the battle of the long haul that was before her. She had to face the trials of caring for someone who would be dependent on her. This would extend over a long time.

It was time to look at the restaurant, her business, and the needs of the house. All of these responsibilities hovered over her head, waiting to crash down upon her shoulders. Clarice was so very tired, yet she believed she had no time to be tired. Subconsciously she shifted into mental overtime. She began using up energy reserves that naturally she did not have. There was only one place to go for help, and that was to the one who had sustained her, upheld her, and answered her every prayer. She went to the Lord for strength. She knew very well that her survival was linked to her ability to stay beneath the shadow of the Almighty. Her source was God, and she needed to stay close to him, now more than ever.

Clarice had friends—the best friends that any person could have—but they could only strengthen and help her so much. When all was said and done and she was pushed to the very limit of human endurance, it was God who showed up and provided the answers. Like Ronnie, she knew that she was under the care of her Heavenly Father.

Clarice became busier than ever as she returned to her personal and business responsibilities. Still her primary responsibility was Ronnie. In some ways, her life became like a circus act. She was spinning plates and balancing days. She had much to accomplish. With her intense schedule, she was always weary. She wanted to pray, but even when she found time to be alone, she was tired. She could hardly concentrate, but she never ceased to say thank you to the Lord, and in doing so she drew strength from him. The quiet moments with the Lord would refuel her engines. She cherished those moments and took them as often as she could.

She talked to the Lord while driving the car, eating meals, and organizing her home. She sat at the end of the day in the dark and lifted her hands to God. How good he had been and how blessed she was to have come through this awful nightmare. The Lord ministered to her like he did to Jesus in the wilderness. He covered her with his wings.

When a crisis moves on and visible miracles cease, people are forced to return to their everyday lives. It is then they must know the resident, abiding peace of God. It is often the uneventful stages of life that produce the success stories of great men and women. The accomplishments that come from days of responsible, routine lifestyles produce fruit, and the accumulation of good fruit yields a bountiful harvest over the years. Sometimes that daily walk of obedience to God produces results that change the world. It releases the provisions and purposes of God, creating a legacy that is passed on to generations to come. The adage is true: "The monumental is often hidden in the mundane."

The tests of life are not only found in the miraculous moments of life where we triumph over adversity and survive unexpected trauma. Tests are also in the day-to-day responsibilities of godly living. If we seek God, follow his will, and consistently serve him, then our path becomes clearer. Each passing season allows character to be formed, purpose to be defined, and direction to be established.

After twelve days at the rehab center, it was time for Ronnie to leave the hospital and be carried home. He had been there for fifty-two days. He could barely move his body, but the remainder of his rehabilitation would happen at home. He was glad, and Clarice was glad to have him. With a heart full of thanksgiving and faith for the future, Ronnie was wheeled down the hospital hallway with Clarice at his side toward the front doors.

Chapter 13

Triumphant Reentry

R onnie Holden was the talk of the town. It is difficult to hide a spectacular story like his from running the grapevine. That was especially true in a small community like Shallotte, where people were well-posted on the daily progress of Ronnie's miraculous recovery. They followed its every step and grew to love Ronnie. He was like a local sport celebrity who had become famous in the major leagues or a war hero who was returning home from the front.

He was returning to Shallotte, and people were proud that he was their friend and brother. Many townspeople knew that this was the day Ronnie would be leaving the hospital. Even the sheriff offered to provide an escort for the journey. He said, "Ronnie Holden is very precious cargo, so please let me do this." Clarice and Ronnie thought it a bit much and turned the offer down.

At first, Ronnie did not want to go home. He was frightened of reentry. He felt so utterly helpless, because he could hardly move his body. He feared the challenge of trying to function at home without the assistance of the hospital staff. The idea of resuming his life was overwhelming. Clarice had a difficult time convincing him that she could and would take care of him. Many other people offered help as well, but Ronnie felt insecure. It took days of spiritual and mental preparation, but once again the Holy Spirit comforted Ronnie, increasing his faith.

Then Ronnie put his trust in the Lord.

The Holdens were not alone. When they wheeled Ronnie into the reception area by the front doors, he was met by a small crowd of hospital workers who had been waiting for him. Before him were doctors, nurses, physiotherapists, secretaries, hospital cleaning staff, patients, and even some people who were visiting other patients. They had all come to send Ronnie off, and they followed him toward the doors, clapping as they went.

As Ronnie's chair rolled past the front doors and out to the covered driveway, Ronnie heard a congregation of birds chirping in the trees by the front of the hospital. He thought it was the most beautiful thing he had ever heard and later said that God set the birds in place and had them sing their very best, just for him. He tried to look up to see them but was struck by the brightness of the day. He squinted to protect his eyes from the sunlight. That is probably why, at first, he did not see where the other singing was coming from. It had just begun, and there were no instruments playing, only a wonderful voice as clear as crystal. It caught his attention because the pitch was solid, and the sound was strong and perfectly smooth.

He slowly shifted his eyes to the side and strained to see beyond the bars of his halo. There, thirty feet away, standing on the sidewalk was a black lady. Her arms were stretched in front of her, and she was leaning back and looking up into the clouds, singing with all of her might. Ronnie realized that her song was in honor of him, and he motioned to his niece's husband to stop pushing his wheelchair for a moment. His heart filled with emotion as the words and tune rolled over him like a shower of warm water. The soloist was hitting the highest notes and sustaining them and adding creative variations to the tune. It gave Ronnie goose bumps on the back of his neck, but it was the words that really broke through.

"Amazing grace! How sweet the sound
that saved a wretch like me!
I once was lost, but now am found;
Was blind, but now I see."

Doctors and nurses began wiping the tears from the corners of their eyes as the Spirit of God moved over the crowd. The song had been rightly sung by millions of individuals before as a tribute to God for saving and rescuing them from their darkest hours. At this moment, however, it was being sung just for Ronnie. Regardless of how many times the tune had been raised as a flag of triumph, this time it was being raised for him. It was sung for the triumph of Ronnie's life. This was his day, and if "Amazing Grace" had been written for him and was never sung for anyone else, if its sole purpose were to amplify the blessing that had come to Ronnie, it would not have been wasted.

Ronnie cried. The doctors cried, and so did the nurses and the hospital workers. There was not a dry eye in that congregation. Every soul was touched by the awesome grace of God. Many of these professionals had not expected Ronnie to survive. Some had insisted that he would die because of what they knew in their fields of medicine. One by one they had been proven wrong, and they were glad. All of them knew the words to "Amazing Grace," but today they stood in witness to the reality of that grace.

The song was a signature at the end of a passionate letter sent from heaven. It captured the theme of Ronnie's epic story. God loves people, and his grace had been lavished on Ronnie. An act of human kindness softens hearts, but God's kindness is overwhelming. His mercy and grace reach the hardest soul and turns a sinner from his ways. Miracles came to Ronnie because of God's love and kindness, but another miracle was at work in the crowd. As they listened to the song, their hearts opened. Faith rushed into every soul. Over the years, many had lost their faith, but on that day, it came rushing back.

"Through many dangers, toils and snares,
I have already come;
'Tis grace hath brought me safe thus far,
and grace will lead me home."

It was a beautiful moment, one that will never be forgotten, but it was no tender moment trying to get Ronnie into the truck. His limp body, colostomy bag, and protruding halo seemed to present an impossible situation. He could not walk, so he had to be carried. Finally they lifted, pushed, and pulled him onto the seat of the GMC pickup. It had headroom and large doors to allow him to get in and pillows in place to prop him up. Ronnie was strapped in and on his way home.

The crowd outside the hospital had grown. The doctors and nurses cheered and waved, wiping tears from their eyes as the truck pulled away. It sounded like a victory celebration after the winning goal of a championship game. It was even better than that, however, because in this case, everybody won.

Jamie Milliken, Ronnie's niece's husband, drove the truck, and another vehicle followed. Soon the horns were honking as if they had come from a wedding. This was the reuniting of a married couple. In his own style of humor, Ronnie thought, "I'll be romantic and carry Clarice over the threshold when I reach the house." He was happy to be going home, but in truth he was the one who would have to be carried over the threshold.

As the small convoy turned onto Shallotte's Main Street, a surprise awaited Ronnie. He recognized friends and supporters waving from the sidewalk. The driver took his time, going extra slow as if driving a float in the Rose Parade.

The people at Shallotte Electric made a special effort to announce Ronnie's return. Employees and friends gathered in front of the business. Children were holding balloons, and young people were waving flags and banners. Some were holding signs to cheer Ronnie on. They were clapping and shouting, "Welcome home, Ronnie." Some were yelling, "Praise the Lord," and, "We love you, Ronnie," and even, "Three cheers for the Miracle Boy."

A church sign read, "Welcome Home Ronnie." Welcome signs for Ronnie were posted on church service announcement boards. Ronnie's homecoming was not just a celebration for him and Clarice, it was a celebration for his friends, his prayer partners, and his neighbors as well.

In ancient times, a conquering military hero would return home to the capital of his country. He would lead a triumphal parade into the city. He rode his chariot, followed by his troops, and displayed his trophies behind him for the crowds to see. He showed off the spoils and wealth he had taken from his enemies. Lastly, his prisoners would be seen walking in chains at the back of the line. The people of the city would cheer and celebrate the victory of their champion.

This convoy of friends was Ronnie's triumphal parade. Unlike the military generals of the past, he had not planned this processional. It was a total surprise. Others who recognized Ronnie's victory had organized his homecoming, and angels were assigned as escorts on parade duty. Ronnie had fought death and triumphed. It was no small matter. Now he was riding into the city in a modern-day chariot for all to see.

This was a military victory of spiritual proportions. The troops were the prayer warriors, hospital workers, and angels. The trophy of the day was Ronnie himself. He was returning from the battlefield. He was being carried along the road. His life, his soul, his body were trophies of God's grace.

The scene calls to mind the scripture:

"Thanks be to God, who always leads us in triumphal procession in Christ and through us spreads everywhere the fragrance of the knowledge of him." 2 Cor. 2:14 NIV

Ronnie's battle was as real as any where guns and grenades are fired. His enemy was just as real as any terrorist or tyrant. Satan was Ronnie's mortal enemy, and he is our enemy as well. He comes to steal, to kill, and to destroy, but God comes to rescue and protect. He comes to give life. It is just as the scripture says:

"The thief comes only to steal and kill and destroy; I have come that they might have life and have it to the full."
John 10:10 NIV

Satan had stolen Ronnie's life. He was destroying him physically and doing all within his power to kill him. The armies of the Lord, both human and angelic, rose to the occasion. They fought the battle and took back what Satan had stolen.

This was God's triumph. It was a triumph for the medical staff of New Hanover Hospital, for the people of God, for angels, and for the town of Shallotte. Many in the crowd had participated in the battle by praying for Ronnie. Some were involved in casual prayers, but many were on the front lines, battling under extended seasons of prayer. The word of the Lord is true. The people of God will fight the enemies of God as he leads them into battle. The scripture says:

"The people who know their God shall be strong, and carry out great exploits." Dan. 11:32 New King JamesVersion

The members of East Side Church had resisted the devil and now were celebrating the answers to their prayers. They had risen to the challenge, and God blessed them in an extraordinary way. It is one thing to hear about miracles that happen in faraway places, but it is quite different when we are personally involved. That was the blessing for the members of East Side. They cried, they prayed, and they had their faith tested. They wrestled over the life of one so close to them. They did not stand in the shadows or run from the day of battle. They stood their ground and fought. They endured the battle through the long dark hours of the night, and they won the victory. They lived out the very words of the Lord in Psalm 126:5, 6 NIV.

"Those who sow in tears will reap with songs of joy. He who goes out weeping, carrying seed to sow, will return with songs of joy, carrying sheaves with him."

The victory over Ronnie's life brought the church members to a new level of faith. It crystallized the word of God in their hearts. The church was never the same again. This experience brought them to new ground, God-given ground that no one could take from them.

When Ronnie rode up the long drive to his house, there were balloons and streamers everywhere. About thirty-five people were at his home to welcome him and help him settle in. What a party followed, and what a blessing it was to be loved by so many. Their friend Randy had ramps built everywhere for Ronnie's wheelchair and had set up a room designed for Ronnie.

Five days a week for the next three months the physiotherapist would come to work with Ronnie. Some basic equipment had been placed in the room for those visits. A bed was set beside Ronnie's so Clarice could sleep close by her husband in case he cried out during the night. The room included as much as possible to be serviceable for Ronnie.

It was Friday afternoon when Ronnie arrived home. After a brief visit with friends, he became weary, and one-by-one his company left. Clarice was alone with Ronnie, and she prepared herself for their first night together at home. A nurse was scheduled to come, but she had not arrived, and Clarice was anxious. She had received no instructions on how to care for Ronnie. She was particularly worried about changing his colostomy bag and did not know what she would do if Ronnie needed to be moved. The nurse was to bring that kind of information and explain to Clarice what her new responsibilities were. The nurse did not show up that first night. It was rough, very rough.

Ronnie's colostomy bag came loose and made an awful mess. Ronnie is six feet tall, and Clarice had no way of moving him. In his condition, he was like dead weight. He was lying on his right side where the friends had left him. She tried earnestly to reach across his body to get the bag back in place. Ronnie became frustrated. It seemed that his worst fears about coming home were being realized. Clarice became nervous and upset. She began to cry. To make matters worse, she slipped while trying to fix his bag and accidentally sat down on Ronnie's broken leg. Pain shot through Ronnie's body, and now both of them were crying. What a mess they were in. They persevered and worked through the ordeal. Somehow they got through that awful first night.

Eventually Clarice received instructions from the nurse. The health-care workers came, and one became a regular help. Her name was Ginny, and she was seventy-five years old. For two months she came two or three times every day. She would pray and have fellowship with Ronnie while she was working with him. Another person who visited regularly was Danny, a Costa Rican pastor. He was working as an assistant pastor at East Side Church and took it upon himself to minister to Ronnie. Ronnie loved this, because Danny would preach his sermons in full to him. Danny had a captive audience. On many occasions Danny's sermons were exactly what Ronnie needed to hear. The Holy Spirit moved in those meetings, and the resulting prayer continued to release healing for Ronnie. They also called upon God for the needs of others, and God heard and answered their prayers.

Although he continued to face new challenges each day, Ronnie slowly got better, and life at home improved. Over the next three months, he visited the hospital ten times and underwent three more operations. A month after that he had his colostomy removed and his halo taken off. At the same time, his walking became noticeably better. He took a full twenty steps using a walker. Those walks were so arduous that sweat poured off his body, and the pain was excruciating. Ronnie was a fighter and simply would not give up. Clarice fought each battle with him. They climbed each physical and mental mountain that rose before them, and things got better.

The entire experience, from Ronnie's accident through his rehabilitation, drew him and Clarice closer together. Their love for each other leaped forward to a special level. They are now inseparable and are a living example of the scripture in Ecclesiastes 4:9–12 NIV.

> *"Two are better than one, because they have a good return for their work: If one falls down, his friend can help him up. But pity the man who falls and has no one to help him up! Also, if two lie down together, they will keep warm. But how can one keep warm alone? Though one may be overpowered, two can defend themselves. A cord of three strands is not quickly broken."*

Ronnie and Clarice were tested in the fires of adversity, and because of those fires, they share many powerful testimonies. Here are five ways that connect Ronnie and Clarice to the truths of Ecclesiastes 4:9–12. Two are better than one.

They labored and still work together diligently in their business and have a good return for their work.

They experienced the trauma of falling into the deepest ditch where even the demons of death came to destroy them. Their outstanding friends, however, helped them to get out of the ditch and up on their feet again.

They kept each other warm in body, soul, and spirit with

unsurpassed loyalty, encouragement, and love.

They were overpowered by the devil, and yet they defended each other. When Ronnie became helpless because of his accident, Clarice rose to defend him valiantly.

They have a powerful, third strand in their cord. Above all other these things, they were and are never alone. Beyond the help of friends and each other, they have God in their lives. He was the awesome third strand in their cord, and a cord of three strands is not quickly broken. With God's help, their rope endured the pull. It did not break when the pressures of life came to attack them. They were not broken, for the Lord sustained them, blessed them, and answered their prayers. He gave them miracles. They received physical healing with many supernatural signs and wonders.

Today, only a few years after Ronnie's accident, they are sailing high in the goodness of God's love. As they operate their business, worship the Lord at church meetings, or walk hand in hand along the beach, it is difficult to know that they have faced such pressing battles. They look wonderful. The glow on their faces and the joy in their hearts might lead one to believe that they never had a difficult day in their lives. Ronnie is well. He is up and about like any normal man, and there is certainly no brain damage. He is a sharp, successful businessman. Together they continue to search out the ways of the Lord. They are ready at any moment to tell some soul of God's abundant love and grace.

Although the particulars are different, the blessing of God on Ronnie and Clarice Holden remind one of God's blessings that came to Job after his great crisis. These are the kind of blessings that the Lord desires to give to all of his children.

"After Job had prayed for his friends, the Lord made him prosperous again and gave him twice as much as he had before…. The Lord blessed the latter part of Job's life more

than the first. He had fourteen thousand sheep, six thousand camels, a thousand yoke of oxen and a thousand donkeys. And he also had seven sons and three daughters. … After this, Job lived a hundred and forty years; he saw his children and their children to the fourth generation. And so he died, old and full of years." Selections from Job 42:10–17 NIV

ADDITIONAL TEACHING

The second part of this book is a series of teachings taken from Bible stories. Each reveals a desperate situation in the lives of troubled people. I am aware that many reading this book will be facing great personal challenges. The subject of fighting death is not everyone's battle at this time, so I felt it was appropriate to address a few other themes. The stories in Part Two give some insights regarding other desperate battles. You may wish to read through each of them or refer to the Table of Contents and read those chapters that apply to your situation. In either case, I trust the stories will encourage and bless you. They are Bible stories and, like the story of Ronnie and Clarice, they are true in every detail.

Part Two

Bible Stories of Desperate People

Chapter 14

Supplication

From the days of the first family, men and women have faced crises and called on the name of the Lord. Right now people in every nation are in desperate need of God's help, and many are praying for mercy. Some are praying for healing, others for family or friends. Some are praying for their church, city, country, or a foreign mission field. You may be facing a hopeless situation and be praying desperately for a miracle.

Miracles happen often. Many times they come in response to desperate prayers. I trust that through these writings you will be inspired and instructed by the Holy Spirit. May you see miracles in answer to your own desperate prayers.

SUPPLICATION

The biblical word for desperate prayer is supplication. It may be defined as, "A desperate cry to God for a miracle in a time of great crisis."

Supplication involves our emotions, humility, sincerity, the will of God, and the special leading of the Holy Spirit. The Bible gives many examples of desperate prayer. A few of them include: Hannah crying to God for a son; Jacob wrestling with the angel for blessings before facing his estranged brother; Jonah crying for deliverance from the belly of the great fish; Esau earnestly seeking repentance that he would not find; Paul crying to be rid of his thorn in the flesh; and Jesus in the garden of Gethsemane asking God to save him from the cross. We will study these and other biblical examples to discover some key ingredients for successful supplication.

JACOB GOES INTO PANIC

For twenty years Jacob looked over his shoulder to see if Esau were there. His brother had promised to kill him. Jacob had bought Esau's birthright, stole his blessing, and fled to their Uncle Laban's house to escape wrath and vengeance.

He married Leah and Rachel, fathered twelve sons, and became independently wealthy. He had household servants, hundreds of sheep, goats, camels, donkeys, and cattle, and he had gained great respect in the community. Regardless of all of these blessings, he was not happy. He had lost favor with Uncle Laban and Laban's sons. They were jealous of his wealth. Moreover, Jacob wanted what he thought he would never be able to have. He wanted to return to his homeland and be reunited with his estranged brother, Esau. Then God spoke to Jacob saying:

"Go back to the land of your fathers and to your relatives, and I will be with you." Gen. 31:3 NIV

He gathered his tribe and commissioned his servants to take all of their belongings, including his flocks and herds, to begin the journey back to his brother. They traveled for weeks until they came within days of Esau's home. Jacob sent a scout ahead of him to his brother's house. The servant was instructed to say that Jacob had been at Uncle Laban's all of these years and was now returning home. He was coming as Esau's servant, with great wealth, hoping to find favor with his brother. The servant returned and told Jacob that Esau was riding out to meet him accompanied by four hundred men.

"In great fear and distress Jacob divided the people.... He thought, 'If Esau comes and attacks one group, the group that is left may escape.'" Gen. 32:7, 8 NIV

Jacob was afraid, and in desperate supplication he called upon God for a miracle. He prayed earnestly, reminding God of his covenant and calling on him for mercy. Then he sent a gift ahead to give to his brother Esau. He sent 550 animals—sheep, goats, camels, donkeys, and cattle—in five herds. He spaced them out, so that Esau would receive them one herd at a time.

He was so desperate that he spent the night alone in prayer. The angel of the Lord appeared to him, and Jacob wrestled with him.

"So Jacob was left alone, and a man wrestled with him till daybreak. When the man saw that he could not overpower him, he touched the socket of Jacob's hip so that his hip was wrenched as he wrestled with the man. Then the man said, 'Let me go, for it is daybreak.' But Jacob replied, 'I will not let you go unless you bless me.' The man asked him, 'What is your name?' 'Jacob,' he answered. Then the man said, 'Your name will no longer be Jacob, but Israel, because you have struggled with God and with men and have overcome.' ... So Jacob called the place Peniel saying, 'It is because I saw God face to face, and yet my life was spared.' " Genesis 32:24–30 NIV

The following day Jacob met Esau. All was forgiven, and the brothers were peacefully reunited.

Here is the essence of supplication. Jacob was in a desperate situation and needed a miracle. He prayed, and God sent his angel who wrestled with him. Jacob fought the battle and prevailed. He prayed and would not let the Lord go until he blessed him.

It is the desperate situation that reveals whether we will wrestle and win or simply give up. God is looking for the warrior in us. He is drawing us out of our comfort zones to fight for that which is valuable.

The results are remarkable. Our names and our character are changed. God's favor and blessings fall on us with miraculous signs and wonders. We have a new testimony of God's love and power, and it remains on us as a banner over our lives. We become meek because of the close encounter with God's power, so from that day on we walk with a limp. We are not arrogant but are humbled by the fear of God.

This is the pathway of desperate prayer. The next few chapters tell Bible stories of desperate people who pressed through and won the blessings and favor of God. May your name be added to the list of victorious people—those who wrestled with God through the dark night until the break of day.

Chapter 15

Desperate Prayer Turns Death Away

King Hezekiah was only thirty-seven years old when he became ill to the point of death. He had served the Lord faithfully. For twelve years he was king of Israel, and it did not seem right that he should die so young. To add insult to injury, Isaiah the prophet came to visit him and left him with bad news. He said,

"This is what the Lord says: Put your house in order, because you are going to die; you will not recover." 2 Kings 20:1 NIV

This felt like a dreadful interruption of King Hezekiah's life. He had reached the pinnacle of success with dignity and virtue. He had become rich and famous. His life had purpose and meaning, and he was known far and wide as a good king. For all intents and purposes, he had done everything right. There is a time when people should die—when they are old and well-advanced in years and have lived a full life; then it seems right that they should go and be with the Lord. For them death is not a sting but a victory. They simply fall asleep and wake in the arms of Jesus. Hezekiah, however, was too young. He was in his prime. Why should he have his life cut short? It felt like he was being punished, and the question why must have haunted him.

Everything was going wrong for Hezekiah, and nothing made sense. This scenario often happens when death looms before good people. We reach to find words of comfort for those who will be left behind. Common words of comfort include: "God picks the best flowers first," or, "They proved their value to God, and so he took them," or, "It was their time," or, "They are in a better place now." All of these words may be true, but they seldom remove the pain or the questions that taunt their loved ones. The scriptures inform us that sometimes people are taken to spare them the pain of upcoming evil. Isaiah 57:1 NIV says:

"The righteous perish, and no one ponders it in his heart; devout men are taken away, and no one understands that the righteous are taken away to be spared from evil."

We often do not understand the battle with death, but scripture calls death our last enemy. If death is our enemy, then he is God's enemy. We should, therefore, fight death with everything we have. If God does not tell us that this death is from him, then we should stand up and fight it with every means possible. Let us settle the issue right now—fight death until God says otherwise.

Hezekiah was in a difficult place. God had spoken and told him he would die and not recover. He was even instructed to put his house in order. He was told to settle his affairs, his estate, and his will. He should appoint his successor and say goodbye to friends and loved ones. It was good advice, but Hezekiah did not have peace about it. He did not think that he should die, and he fought back with desperate prayer.

"Hezekiah turned his face to the wall and prayed to the Lord, 'Remember, O Lord, how I have walked before you faithfully and with wholehearted devotion and have done what is good in your eyes.' And Hezekiah wept bitterly." 2 Kings 20:2–3 NIV

Then God sent Isaiah back to King Hezekiah with this message.

> *"This is what the Lord ... says: I have heard your prayers and seen your tears; I will heal you.... I will add fifteen years to your life."* 2 Kings 20:5–6 NIV

God healed Hezekiah even though he had prophesied his death. He heard his cry, saw his tears, and granted Hezekiah his wish. There are some details surrounding this miracle that are worth mentioning. God gave Hezekiah instructions of a medical nature, and he gave him a supernatural sign. The miraculous sign from God was necessary to inspire faith, because it was vital that Hezekiah stand in faith before the miracle could happen. It was also important that Hezekiah obey the medical instruction he was given.

> *"Then Isaiah said, 'Prepare a poultice of figs.' They did so and applied it to the boil, and he recovered."* 2 Kings 20:7 NIV

Boils were commonplace in biblical times. They are painful, but they do not cause death. I am sure that it was not a common boil that threatened Hezekiah's life, or a poultice of figs that cured him. It was obedience and faith in response to God's word that healed Hezekiah. Here is a biblical example, however, where divine healing did not exclude medical remedies. God will often use doctors and medical procedures when he heals someone.

Hezekiah asked the prophet for a miraculous sign from God. He knew he needed faith to set his mind at rest. He needed a sign to help him stand in full assurance of the coming miracle. It is not wrong to ask God for a sign; in fact it was part of the healing process.

"Isaiah answered, 'This is the Lord's sign to you that the Lord will do what he has promised: Shall the shadow go forward ten steps, or shall it go back ten steps?' ' It is a simple matter for the shadow to go forward ten steps,' said Hezekiah. 'Rather, have it go back ten steps.' Then the prophet Isaiah called upon the Lord, and the Lord made the shadow go back the ten steps it had gone down on the stairs of Ahaz." 2 Kings 20:9–11 NIV

It was the end of the day when shadows lengthen, but a miraculous sign was given for Hezekiah's benefit—the shadow shortened. After already lengthening down ten steps, it reversed and went ten steps back, as Hezekiah had asked. Signs and wonders often accompany healing miracles.

Chapter 16

Desperate Prayer Raises the Dead

GOOD PEOPLE HAVE TROUBLES

A wealthy woman from Shunem invited Elisha for a meal, because she recognized him as a man of God. Her husband did not appear to be a spiritual man but agreed to make a special room on the roof of their house where Elisha could stay when he was in town.

After visiting a few times and receiving the hospitality of the couple, Elisha asked what he could do for them. They asked for nothing, but Elisha insisted, and Gehazi, Elisha's servant, said:

"Well, she has no son. ..." 2 Kings 4:14 NIV

Elisha called the woman:

" 'About this time next year," Elisha said, 'you will hold a son in your arms.' 'No, my lord,' she objected. 'Don't mislead your servant, O man of God!' " 2 Kings 4:16 NIV

One year later, the woman gave birth to a son, and the child became the joy and delight of their home. When he was a young

[119]

boy, he went out to the field where his father was reaping and became ill. He complained of great pain in his head, and a servant carried him to his mother. The boy sat on his mother's lap until noon and then died.

Immediately the woman carried him up the stairs to the prophet's chamber and laid him on the bed. She did not let her husband know what had happened, perhaps because he was not a man of faith. She commanded her servant to take her to Mount Carmel with all haste to see Elisha, the man of God.

Elisha saw her approaching and sent Gehazi to inquire of her need. She did not tell him, but when she came to Elisha, she took hold of his feet and cried out.

The scripture says she was in bitter distress.

> " 'Did I ask you for a son, my lord?' she said. 'Didn't I tell you, "Don't raise my hopes"?' " 2 Kings 4:28 NIV

URGENT INSTRUCTIONS

Gehazi was instructed to run to her house and place the prophet's staff on the boy's body and face. He was not to stop, meet, or even greet anyone on the way. It was a matter of great urgency, and the prophet's instructions were vital.

The Shunammite woman refused to leave Elisha's side, and together they proceeded to her house. When they arrived, the boy was still dead. Elisha's staff seemed to make no difference. Elisha went into the room alone and shut the door. He prayed, but nothing happened.

> "Then he got on the bed and lay upon the boy, mouth to mouth, eyes to eyes, hands to hands. As he stretched himself out upon him, the boy's body grew warm." 2 Kings 4:34 NIV

Still the boy did not return to life, and Elisha got off the bed and began praying again.

"Elisha turned away and walked back and forth in the room and then got back on the bed and stretched out upon him once more. The boy sneezed seven times and opened his eyes. She [the Shunammite woman] came in, fell at his feet and bowed to the ground. Then she took her son and went out." 2 Kings 4:35–37 NIV

When the boy died, the woman knew exactly where to find help. She needed the power of God, and nothing else would bring her son back to life. She did not tell her plan to her husband, her servant, or even Gehazi, the prophet's servant. Perhaps they would not have stood in faith, and she needed the prayer of agreement, not doubt.

Elisha prayed desperately. He listened to the Holy Spirit. He not only stretched himself over the body of the boy but stretched his faith beyond the realm of nature. He supplicated and desperately called upon the Lord for a miracle, and God granted his request. The word of God is true.

"The effective fervent prayer of a righteous man avails much."
James 5:16 NKJV

GOD HEARS A DESPERATE WIDOW

A similar story is told of Elijah, who was Elisha's mentor. It begins with a meeting that was set up by God. The Lord instructed Elijah to go to Zarephath. He said, "I have commanded a widow in that place to supply you with food."

Now the widow had next to nothing, but God was at work, because he had heard her desperate prayer. Elijah saw the widow gathering sticks and asked her for a drink of water. As she was getting a drink for him, he called and asked her for a piece of bread as well.

"As surely as the Lord your God lives," she replied, "I don't have any bread—only a handful of flour in a jar and a little oil in a jug. I am gathering a few sticks to take home and make a meal for myself and my son, that we may eat it—and die." 1 Kings 17:12 NIV

Elijah, nevertheless, continued to ask the woman to make him a cake of bread and then to make one for herself and her son. There was a drought in the land, and Elijah told her that God would replenish her flour and oil supernaturally until the rains came. The miracle happened, just as the prophet said.

"So there was food every day for Elijah and for the woman and her family. For the jar of flour was not used up and the jug of oil did not run dry, in keeping with the word of the Lord spoken by Elijah." 1 Kings 17:15–16 NIV

THE SON DIED

Some time later the son of the woman became sick. He grew worse and worse until he stopped breathing and died.

"She said to Elijah, 'What do you have against me, man of God? Did you come to remind me of my sin and kill my son?' " 1 Kings 17:18 NIV

Elijah took the boy to the upper room in the house where he was staying and laid him on his bed. Then he prayed desperately.

"Then he cried out to the Lord, 'O Lord my God, have you brought tragedy also upon this widow I am staying with, by causing her son to die?' Then he stretched himself out on the boy

three times and cried to the Lord, 'O Lord my God, let this boy's life return to him.' The Lord heard Elijah's cry, and the boy's life returned to him, and he lived." 1 Kings 17:20–22 NIV

God was interested in preserving his prophet, but he also was interested in blessing the poor widow. He brought them together, fed them supernaturally, and healed her bitter heart. It is most likely that the boy had a disease all along. Perhaps even a demon of premature death was at work in him because of an ancestral curse. When it manifested, God made sure that a fighter was present. Elijah, the man of God, was that fighter. He did not give up. He supplicated with desperate prayer over and over again, and God brought life back into the boy. I believe God healed and delivered the boy, in addition to raising him from the dead.

From that day forward, the widow lived in faith. In her early years, she had lived a life of sin and believed that her pains were the judgments and punishments of God. Deep inside, she probably blamed him rather than the devil for her sorrows.

Through the miracle of provision and the resurrection of her son, the widow was healed emotionally. She gained faith and knew that the God of Israel was trustworthy and true (1 Kings 17:24).

MODERN-DAY RESURRECTIONS

Over the last few years, I have heard of several resurrections. I have talked with people who were directly involved in the details of these miracles. I have personally prayed and witnessed a man come to life after he was dead. The man who was resurrected in my presence not only came back to life but was healed of heart disease, high cholesterol, and back problems at the same time. We give God all the praise, for he is the one who performed the miracle. God still heals people and performs extraordinary miracles today just as he did thousands of years ago.

Chapter 17

Desperate Prayer Serves the Lord

I WANT A BABY

Hannah had no children and lived in remorse and shame because of it. In her culture and time, not having children was a desperate matter. Children were a sign of God's favor and a demonstration of true wealth. They were the continuation of a family bloodline and a gift in one's old age. Without children, one may have felt forsaken by God, stricken by poverty, and even cursed.

God was not going to leave Hannah in this childless condition, but he had a larger purpose for her life, one greater than she could imagine. Often we are not aware of God's design for our lives. Subsequently, we do not understand how necessary our personal struggle might be. Life may feel like an eternal detour, but if we walk with the Lord, he will not lead us astray. God is always at work to perform his will, and that was why Hannah faced such a battle to conceive a child. She was unaware of the greater purposes of God, and, therefore, she thought he had forsaken her. In fact, he was working with her from the start.

At this time in Israel's history, Eli the priest was God's representative. Unfortunately, he had left the path of godliness. His sons were committing adultery with the women who came to the temple to pray, and Eli would not correct them. Sin was rampant in high places, and spiritual doors were open for demonic activity to flourish throughout the country. This is a spiritual principle. If those in authority sin, it releases a trickle-down effect for sin to be multiplied among the subordinates. This was destroying the people of Israel and hindering the flow of blessings that God had promised to them and the entire world. Through Abraham's seed, all the nations would be blessed but not unless there was massive change.

The Lord was at work in Hannah to bring them back on course. He needed a leader who would put his people on track and close the demonic door of destruction over the nation.

Hannah did not see the larger picture. She just wanted a child, and she was desperate. She probably asked the Lord what she had done wrong or what further criteria she must meet to gain God's favor. Hannah's sin, however, was not the problem. She cried desperately for God to bless her, but nothing seemed to work.

If we are doing all we can to please the Lord and still cannot find good results, it is time to pray in faith, trust the Lord, and get desperate. Hannah was in the middle of a wearisome ordeal, but God was drawing her to a place of ultimate sacrifice. At the peak of her frustration and despair, she went to the temple to pray. In desperation, she promised that if God gave her a son, she would give him back to the Lord.

"In bitterness of soul Hannah wept much and prayed to the Lord. And she made a vow, saying, 'O Lord Almighty, if you will only look upon your servant's misery ... and give her a son, then I will give him to the Lord for all the days of his life....' Eli observed her mouth. Hannah was praying in her heart, and her lips were moving but her voice was not heard. Eli thought she was drunk and said to her, 'How long will you

*keep on getting drunk? Get rid of your wine.' 'Not so, my
lord,' Hannah replied, 'I am a woman who is deeply troubled.... I was pouring out my soul to the Lord.... I have been
praying here out of my great anguish and grief.' Eli answered,
'Go in peace, and may the God of Israel grant you what you
have asked of him.' So in the course of time Hannah conceived and gave birth to a son.... After he was weaned, they
brought the boy to Eli, and she said to him, '... I am the
woman who stood here beside you praying to the Lord. I prayed
for this child, and the Lord has granted me what I asked of
him. So now I give him to the Lord. For his whole life he will
be given over to the Lord....' And he worshipped the Lord
there."* Selections from 1 Sam. 1:10–28 NIV

INDUCED SACRIFICE

It is human nature to live one's life in the pursuit of peace
and comfort. People seldom rise to great sacrifice unless
prompted by strong motivation. It is unlikely that Hannah would
have given her firstborn son to Eli the priest for lifelong service
in the temple if she had not been desperate. Had she not been
pressed, it probably would not have happened. There was a
higher purpose, however, and Hannah was unaware of it.

Out of frustration and at her wits end, she supplicated and
made a vow to God. She promised God that he could have her
son if he would only give her one. The result was greater than
anyone could have imagined. She bore a son and gave him to the
Lord. In doing so, she did not lose a son, but she, and the world,
gained a prophet of the Lord.

A PROPHET IS BORN

The child she gave birth to was Samuel. He was the great
prophet of the Old Testament. The Bible says of him:

"The Lord was with Samuel as he grew up, and he let none of his words fall to the ground. And all Israel ... recognized that Samuel was attested as a prophet of the Lord. The Lord continued to appear... and... revealed himself to Samuel through his word. And Samuel's word came to all Israel."
1 Sam. 3:19–21 and 1 Sam. 4:1 NIV

God was looking for a leader who would restore his people to righteousness, and Samuel was his choice. Samuel anointed David as king, lifted up God's standard for holiness, and brought new direction to the nation. This set the stage for God to bless his people and, in time, to bless the whole world through the coming of Christ. Samuel was a key player in the eternal purposes of God, and Hannah was honored to be his mother.

JESUS WAS DESPERATE

There is no greater example of desperate prayer than that of Jesus before he went to the cross. His disciples had no idea of the higher purpose that God was unfolding through Christ's death. They were bewildered, because they only saw his suffering. Afterward they learned that he died to pay for the sins of the world so that all who believe may come into God's family.

Unlike Hannah, Jesus knew exactly what was before him. He knew why he had to suffer. Even so, he supplicated and cried desperately for help from his Heavenly Father. God heard the desperate prayers of Jesus but did not change his course of action. We read about it in Mark 14:32–36 NIV:

"They went to the place called Gethsemane, and Jesus ... began to be deeply distressed and troubled. 'My soul is overwhelmed with sorrow to the point of death,' he said.... 'Abba, Father,' he said, 'everything is possible for you. Take this cup from me. Yet not what I will, but what you will.'"

EVERY FILTHY SIN

He was preparing to die. The guilt and punishment of every filthy sin was crawling over his soul and lying on him like a million poisonous spiders about to sting. Included were people's secret and hidden sins. Included were the very worst transgressions and iniquities of every human being. From every nation and every generation, they came and fell on him like an avalanche. The wickedness of those sins was more than he wanted to bear. He despised them and scorned the shame of the cross.

"Let us fix our eyes on Jesus, the author and perfecter of our faith, who for the joy set before him endured the cross, scorning its shame.... Consider him who endured ... so that you will not grow weary and lose heart." Heb. 12:2, 3 NIV

The desperate prayers of Jesus were so fervent that sweat dropped like blood from his face. He was in anguish and sorrow, to the point of death. We read in Luke 22: 42–45 NIV:

"'Father, if you are willing, take this cup from me; yet not my will, but yours be done.' An angel from heaven appeared to him and strengthened him. And being in anguish, he prayed more earnestly, and his sweat was like drops of blood falling to the ground."

We read more details of his struggle in Hebrews 5:7, 8 NIV. He cried aloud and tears ran down His face because of the trauma before Him.

"During the days of Jesus' life on earth, he offered up prayers and petitions with loud cries and tears to the one who could save him from death, and he was heard because of his reverent submission. Although he was a son, he learned obedience from what he suffered."

When Jesus prayed these desperate prayers, God heard, and angels attended and comforted him as they did with Ronnie Holden. Nevertheless, God did not release him from the cross. A larger plan was in the making, and Jesus yielded to his Father's will.

NOT JUST FOR LAZARUS

The collateral purpose to our personal crisis may not be as far-reaching as Hannah's. It is certainly not as far-reaching as Christ's. It is, however, still significant. Lazarus became sick and died. His sisters were overwhelmed with grief. Behind his death, a plan was unfolding, and it was extremely important. His death was part one of a two-part story. The second half of the story was his resurrection. His death and resurrection were necessary so that Jesus might be glorified through the miracle, and people might put their faith in him (John 11:4). In Lazarus's case, there was much more at stake than his personal victory. The story of Lazarus has reached every generation in millions of communities around the world. It has been a story that has caused millions to enter the family of God and receive of his blessings.

EVEN A BLIND MAN

A victorious testimony followed the blind man whom Jesus healed. We read the story in John 9:2, 3 NIV:

"His disciples asked him, 'Rabbi, who sinned, this man or his parents, that he was born blind?' 'Neither this man nor his parents sinned,' said Jesus, 'but this happened so that the work of God may be displayed in his life.' "

In the hour of personal pain and crisis we are desperate, and the larger purposes of God are far removed from our thoughts. Those plans, however, are not far from God's thoughts. It is not crucial that we understand what God is up to, but our urgent struggle is always part of something bigger than what we see. Being aware of the larger purpose of God will help us better identify our enemy, use the right weapons to defeat him, and give us wisdom and endurance when we pray.

If you are a Christian and your trauma is not self-inflicted through sin, then there is a higher purpose involved. God is at work in and through you. Like Hannah, Lazarus, or the blind man, you may not know the reason behind the pain, but God has a plan. His word stands true, and you can stand firmly on it. I encourage you to read the following scripture carefully.

> *"The Spirit helps us in our weakness. We do not know what we ought to pray for, but the Spirit himself intercedes for us … because the Spirit intercedes for the saints in accordance with God's will. And we know that in all things God works for the good of those who love him, who have been called according to his purpose. … What, then, shall we say in response to this? If God is for us, who can be against us? He who did not spare his own Son, but gave him up for us all—how will he not also, along with him, graciously give us all things?"*
> Selections from Rom. 8:26–32 NIV

Chapter 18

Desperate Prayers
for Fallen People

RUNNING FROM GOD

Jonah, like each of us, had a call of God on his life. He was asked by the Lord to go to the city of Nineveh to warn them of God's judgment. He did not like the job God had given him, and he ran. He boarded a ship going in the opposite direction. God responded by hurling a massive storm on the sea. The storm was so severe that the sailors thought they would die. Eventually they drew lots and discovered that Jonah was the bad apple in the bunch. Reluctantly they threw him overboard, and he ended up in the belly of a great fish.

He quickly found himself in a desperate, if not hopeless, situation. It was pitch black, and he was lying in gastric juices that were stinging his body and eyes. He was swimming in vomit with seaweed wrapped around his head and bits of fish and guts all around him. No doubt he was nauseous. With the smell and motion of the sea, he had to work hard to keep his head above the fish's stomach fluid just to breathe.

I doubt that anyone reading this has ever been in a situation quite like this. Many a man or woman called to ministry, however, have willfully wandered off track and found themselves in a putrid state. Many have landed in the pigpen like the prodigal son. Jonah began calling out to God from the belly of the fish. He was desperate. He felt that God had forsaken him, but he had nowhere else to go so he prayed:

> *"You hurled me into the deep. … I said, 'I have been banished from your sight; yet I look again toward your holy temple.' … When my life was ebbing away, I remembered you Lord, and my prayer rose to you.… Those who cling to worthless idols forfeit the grace that could be theirs. But I, with a song of thanksgiving, will sacrifice to you. What I have vowed I will make good. … And the Lord commanded the fish, and it vomited Jonah onto dry land."* Selections from Jon. 2:3–4, 7–10 NIV

Jonah was brought to a place of desperate prayer so that God might change him. It was a good thing for Jonah that he was changeable. As strange as it seems, God loved Jonah and did not want him to miss his destiny. God's love for us leads him to extreme measures so that we may fulfill our calling.

A SLOW LEARNER

Jonah was vomited out of the fish onto the beach. He obeyed God, went to Nineveh, and preached repentance to the people. A miracle happened. The people of Nineveh repented. Jonah, however, was a slow learner. He flipped from being a rebel to being a self-righteous legalist in just a few days. God hates rebellion, but he also hates pride and self-righteousness. While we may sin as a rebel and go the way of the world, we may also sin in the middle of church life, through smugness and attitudes of superiority. That is what happened to Jonah.

When the people of Nineveh repented, God poured out his grace upon them. Jonah did not understand that God loves people and delights in blessing them. He knew that the people of

Nineveh did not deserve God's blessings; none of us do. They were in a terrible state of sin, but the fear of God came over them. They entered into desperate prayer and changed their ways. God answered their desperate prayer and blessed them.

When God did not judge Nineveh, Jonah sulked and complained. He wanted to see them burn in the judgments of God—just like it happened in Sodom.

God said to Jonah:

"But Nineveh has more than a hundred and twenty thousand people who cannot tell their right hand from their left, and many cattle as well. Should I not be concerned about that great city?" Jon. 4:11 NIV

In the belly of the fish, Jonah did not believe that God loved him. Neither could Jonah believe that God loved the sinful people of Nineveh. The truth is that God loved Jonah, he loved Nineveh, and he certainly loves you.

Wherever you are coming from, even if you are a man or woman of God who has totally messed up in life, God will hear your desperate prayers if you are serious enough to turn around and change your ways. He did it with Jonah and the people of Nineveh, and he will do it for you.

SELLING OUR SOULS

Sampson was raised to be a man of God, but he forsook the ways of the Lord. He sold his soul for pleasures with the harlot Delilah and paid a heavy price. God gave him superhuman strength and with it a personal secret—he was not to cut his hair. Sampson allowed Delilah to seduce him, and he gave away his secret. She betrayed him. She cut his hair while he was sleeping and called for his enemies to take him. The Spirit of the Lord left him because of his sin. His enemies gouged out his eyes, chained him to a grinding stone at the mill, and made sport of him.

It seemed that all was lost—he had messed up so badly. In the end, however, he had a change of mind. He repented and prayed desperately for God to give him another chance. He had forfeited much of his destiny, but God poured grace upon him and blessed him in the end. He not only went to heaven, but he left the earth in a great victory.

WHAT ABOUT YOU?

If you are facing a desperate crisis and are crying out to God for help, first examine your life. If there is sin, confess and repent. Repenting is being sorry for your actions, but saying you are sorry is not enough. Repentance means to turn around and go in the opposite direction. After repenting of sin, people's lives change, so that sin becomes the exception and not the pattern anymore.

Listen to the scripture.

"If we claim to be without sin, we deceive ourselves and the truth is not in us. If we confess our sins, he is faithful and just and will forgive us our sins and purify us from all unright-eousness." 1 John 1:8, 9 NIV

Pray out loud, in an audible voice. Tell the Lord Jesus that you are sorry for your sin. Ask him to forgive you and be sure to change your behavior. Furthermore, renounce the sins of your forefathers and the sins of your youth. Leave no stone unturned.

God loves you, and it does not matter what you have done. All that matters is your serious decision to turn around and walk with him. If you ask him, he will begin to change you, to protect you, and to use you in his great plan. His angels will come and help you, and he most certainly will answer your desperate prayer.

GRACE IS AN OPPORTUNITY

"But where sin abounded, grace abounded much more." Rom. 5:20 NKJV

Grace is an opportunity. Grace is God's kindness that we cannot deserve. His grace, however, does not come automatically. We must do three things.

1. Believe that God's grace is available to us.
2. Obey the conditions of it.
3. Reach out and receive it.

Then God's grace covers us, and we will be blessed. It is essential that you believe that God loves you not because you accomplish something, but because he loves people, and he created you for fellowship with himself. The primary reason God caused you to be born in this world was to serve him, to be blessed by him, and to be his friend. 1 Peter 3:9 reads:

"For this reason you were called, so that you might inherit a blessing."

By faith, take the opportunity today. Pray the desperate prayer and begin to inherit a blessing.

Chapter 19

Desperate Prayers
That Do Not Work

TRANSGRESSORS

Many people cry to God for mercy when trouble strikes but do not take into account the negative power of unresolved sin. Their path is littered with hardship, because they continue to break God's natural and spiritual laws. That is why the scriptures say, *"The way of transgressors is hard."* Prov. 13:15 KJV

Sin leaves a trail of death: death to our dreams and destiny, death to relationships, and death to our body and soul. The law of sowing and reaping says the way you live will determine the results of your life, whether good or bad. Another way of saying this is that our decisions today determine the quality of our lives tomorrow. Scripture says it like this:

> *"But each one is tempted when, by his own evil desire, he is dragged away and enticed. Then, after desire has conceived, it gives birth to sin; and sin, when it is full-grown, gives birth to death."* James 1:14, 15 NIV

Death can be stopped. Bad results can be reversed but only through repentance, confession, and acceptance of God's grace.

Faith in the sacrifice of Jesus' death on the cross, combined with an uncompromising commitment to follow him, will change everything.

When these principles are not maintained, and God's natural laws are broken, then the body and soul break down. The thief, Satan, and his army of demons have opportunity to come in and steal our hopes, our dreams, and our very life. When we make a deal with him, he takes us where we don't want to go, makes us stay a lot longer than we expected, and makes us pay far more than we can afford.

Listen to the story of Esau, who supplicated and prayed desperately but did not receive God's blessings. The account is given to us in Hebrews 12:14–17 NIV.

> *"Make every effort to live in peace with all men and to be holy; without holiness no one will see the Lord. See to it that no one misses the grace of God and that no bitter root grows up to cause trouble and defile many. See that no one is sexually immoral, or is godless like Esau, who for a single meal sold his inheritance rights as the oldest son. Afterward, as you know, when he wanted to inherit this blessing, he was rejected. He could bring about no change of mind, though he sought the blessing with tears."*

Repentance is not simply saying "sorry." Repentance means turning around and going in the other direction. It involves a different life style. Esau prayed desperately for God's blessing over his life, but his behavior did not change. He said good words but had no change of mind or action. He was an immoral man and a Godless man. His life was one of throwing away God's blessings for momentary pleasure.

Esau sold his birthright and despised his parents' blessings and counsel. Against the laws of God, he married several wives— all of them from the godless cities of Canaan. They were women of witchcraft, involved in idol worship and demonic activity. He wanted the blessings of God, as most people do, but was never prepared to change his way of thinking or his behavior. The scripture defines him as an immoral and godless man.

PAINFUL TO WATCH

The results were painful to watch. It is not that God did not love Esau initially, but that love turned sour, because Esau continued to throw God's grace away. Demons had a field day with him, and God did not protect him, because he continued to invite disaster upon himself.

In the end, he begged God for blessings, he prayed desperately, and he supplicated in anguish, but to no avail, because he would not change his behavior. Desperate prayers do not work simply because they are desperate. Supplication requires a humble attitude, a sincere heart, true repentance, the will of God, and the leading of the Holy Spirit.

THE STEPS OF A GOOD MAN

Every good man or woman will stumble occasionally, perhaps even repeating past failures, but they will repent. After they repent of their sins, their lives change so that sin becomes the exception and not the pattern. This change is facilitated by removing the habits, objects, relationships, and attitudes that promote sin in one's life. In this way, you reinforce your repentance until there is no longer a place for that sin to have dominion over you. God then delights in the ways of that man or woman and makes their steps firm. The scriptures capture the truth of God's mercy for that kind of person. It says in Psalms 37:23, 24 NIV:

> "If the Lord delights in a man's way, he makes his steps firm; though he stumble, he will not fall, for the Lord upholds him with his hand."

No one needs to remain on the road of permanent failure. It is not God's plan or desire that anyone remain unsaved. Help is available for any serious soul. Those who call upon the Lord will be saved. God can change the vilest sinner if that person is willing to let God take control of his life.

If you feel that you fit this chapter, but you do not want to stay here, then go back one step to the previous chapter and follow the direction for desperate prayers for fallen people. If you are serious, you can call upon the Lord, and he will show up.

Chapter 20

Desperate Prayers That Make Us Holy

DISCIPLINE

Some of life's struggles are downloaded on us to discipline us and help us learn obedience. Even Jesus learned obedience from the things he suffered (Heb. 5:8, 9). God insists upon discipline and tells us that we are not his children if we do not experience his correction in our lives (Heb. 12:8). When disciplined by the Lord, we receive his holiness (Heb. 12:10).

THORNS ARE NASTY

The Apostle Paul struggled with a great crisis in his life. He called it a thorn in his flesh, a messenger of Satan sent to torment him. He could not get rid of it. It was God's discipline in his life. He prayed desperately and sought the Lord for deliverance, but God would not pull it out.

"To keep me from becoming conceited because of these surpassingly great revelations, there was given me a thorn in my flesh, a messenger of Satan, to torment me. Three times I pleaded with the Lord to take it away from me. But he said to me, 'My grace is sufficient for you, for my power is made

perfect in weakness. Therefore I will boast all the more gladly about my weaknesses, so that Christ's power may rest on me.'"
2 Cor. 12:7–9 NIV

The Apostle Paul, as great as he was, could not humble himself sufficiently for God's purpose. He needed help from God, so he was given a serious, persistent trauma. Theologians argue over the subject of Paul's thorn in the flesh and cannot come to agreement on what it was. Needless to say, it was very bad. We do know it was considered a thorn.

A thorn is a splinter whose aim in life is to be buried in our flesh to bring us pain. It is excruciating and persists in troubling us until we remove it. Usually we can see only the very end of it. Most of it is hidden from view. Others may not see it at all, but it is always there, annoying us, hurting us, and getting in the way of our peace and progress.

A specific thorn was in Paul's flesh. The biblical use of the word flesh may refer to the physical body or the carnal nature. Paul's trouble could have been a sickness or some bodily weakness that wore him out or disabled him from being his best. Paul was a missionary, and physical sickness is a missionary's nightmare. Missionaries are often traveling on the road or in places of physical hardship that require fortitude and endurance. If his thorn in the flesh was a physical handicap, then Paul would have seen it as a great hindrance to his mission of preaching the gospel.

The other possible thought is that Paul's thorn was a problem in his soul. It may have been a self-defiling temptation that tormented him, a hidden sin that he could not remove. He may have fallen into sin, in his mind, or been subject to loneliness, rejection, or devastating depression. Most people of God have suffered from such attacks. Paul admitted that the things he wanted to do, he did not, and the things he hated to do, he did (Rom. 7:15). He battled with temptation and with making wrong choices. Even a quick tongue may be a thorn in the flesh for some. A quick tongue can hurt friends and drive off acquaintances. Some folks are unable to develop relationships or get close to people because of that thorn in the flesh.

It is humbling when we pray for others and see them healed but suffer from a persistent illness ourselves. It is humbling to counsel others, giving good advice that sets them free, and find that we still struggle with hidden chains of bondage.

We do not know what Paul's thorn in the flesh was, but it was serious. It was a messenger from Satan sent to trouble him. It was not just a hangnail or a bad hair day. He wrestled this demon regularly and could not get rid of it. This thorn in the flesh became Paul's personal challenge and his ongoing trauma.

PAUL'S DESPERATE PRAYER

Three times Paul set himself to prayer so that God would deliver him from this awful affliction. He supplicated and pleaded with the Lord, but nothing happened. He became frustrated. The Lord refused to set him free from this menace, and he let Paul know the reason why.

It was God's will to leave Paul's trouble in place but give him additional grace to bear the torment of it. It seems an awful deal, but God had a larger purpose in mind. It was a necessary evil designed to maintain the supernatural power of miracles in Paul's life and ministry.

Ultimately the power of God that rested on Paul was available only if he could remain humble. Pride is the root of all sin, and everyone has it. It is why God will resist us, and many people will avoid us. One person said, "Pride is like bad breath. You don't know that you have it, but everyone else does."

BLESSINGS OR REJECTION

"God opposes the proud but gives grace to the humble. Humble yourselves, therefore, under God's mighty hand, that he may lift you up in due time." 1 Pet. 5:5, 6 NIV

If God opposes the proud, we must do all within our power to get rid of it. When we are in need of miraculous answers to prayer, it is no time to have God oppose us. That is when we need him the most. We must learn to choose an attitude of humility and, whatever the cost, cut away our pride.

I like the way Derek Prince puts it. He writes: "Our job is to humble ourselves, and God's job is to exalt us, in due time. If we do God's job and exalt ourselves, then he is only left to do our job, and he humbles us." In fact, he humiliates us.

Paul had a blessing that added to his pride. He tells not only of his missionary accomplishments on earth but of his personal visits to heaven as well. He does not claim these experiences as his own, but most theologians argue that he was speaking of himself.

> "I will go on to visions and revelations from the Lord. I know a man ... who was caught up to the third heaven ... was caught up to paradise. He heard inexpressible things that man is not permitted to tell. ... I will not boast about myself.... But I refrain, so no one will think more of me than is warranted. ... To keep me from becoming conceited because of these surpassingly great revelations, there was given me a thorn in my flesh." Selections from 2 Cor. 12:1–7

Paul may have thought that he could have these experiences, and it would not go to his head, but evidently God did not feel the same way. He knew that pride would get the better of Paul—that pride would disqualify him from the power of God. Paul, therefore, had a constant reminder of his personal frailty; he had a thorn in the flesh. He knew that if God did not sustain him, he could not continue in the ministry with great power. This kept him dependent on the Lord. It kept him humble and kept his boast focused on Christ and not on himself.

THEN I AM STRONG

"Three times I pleaded with the Lord to take it away from me. But he said to me, 'My grace is sufficient for you, for my power is made perfect in weakness.' Therefore I will boast all the more gladly about my weakness, so that Christ's power may rest on me. That is why, for Christ's sake, I delight in weaknesses, in insults, in hardships, in persecutions, in difficulties. For when I am weak, then I am strong." 2 Cor. 12:8–10

Miracles flowed as long as Paul was humble. Hardships, insults, persecution, and difficulties made him weak but kept God's power in his life. Perhaps his hallmark statement is, "When I am weak, then I am strong."

Weakness alone does not release God's power. There are many who live in weakness but have no extraordinary power from God. Faith mixed with humility releases the power. Weakness must be accompanied by a right attitude to be transformed into humility. Weakness is external; humility is internal. It is a choice we make.

PAUL'S RECIPE

Paul yielded to God and allowed the weakness in his life to be made into humility. When people hurt him, he did not simply take it like a human punching bag. Paul knew the three-part Bible recipe for personal healing when others betrayed or hurt him. He actively spoke and did what was necessary.

1. He forgave them.
2. He prayed for good to come to them.
3. He blessed them in some practical way.

Then his weakness was turned to humility. Paul also humbled himself by receiving the sacrifices that God placed before him. He endured hardness as a good soldier. He yielded to God's will once he knew what God wanted of him. Sacrifice was not an issue. He learned to embrace hardship and be content in it and, because of it, God was able to bless him.

HUMILITY IS NOT PASSIVE

Humility must not be confused with a passive attitude toward sin or demons. Jesus and Paul cast out demons and renounced sin whenever the Spirit instructed them to minister in that way. Both Jesus and Paul did not only behave as lambs, they knew how to be lions when the situation called for a fight.

Chapter 21

Desperate Prayers
to Save a Nation

NATIONS COMMIT SIN

The Israelites, God's chosen people, fell from the path of godliness into idolatry. King Ahab did more evil in the sight of God than any other Jewish king before him. He was an immoral man, and his sin included marrying the daughter of a demonic priest. Besides being a priest, this man was the king of the Sidonians. His daughter's name was Jezebel. She was a practicing witch. By marrying Ahab, she became queen of Israel. Although Israel was God's chosen nation, Jezebel brought the worship of Baal into the land. This was only possible because King Ahab allowed himself to be seduced by her. Without the weakness of King Ahab, Jezebel could never have brought such evil to the nation. Ahab had a sinful heart and was totally won over by Jezebel's ways. He set up an altar unto Baal and built a temple for him in the city of Samaria. It was during this time of evil that Hiel rebuilt the wicked city of Jericho, against the commandment of God (1 Kings 16:29–34).

Israel, like many nations today, had turned from God to serve idols and worship demons. In those days, idol worship was the outward pattern of worship for false religions. Idol worship is still practiced in many cultures today. In the West, idols are not so recognizable, but they are just as real.

Many God-fearing Jews were desperately praying. God responded to their prayers and raised up a prophet to stand against the demonic stronghold and bring the nation back to the ways of the Lord. The prophet's name was Elijah. God empowered him and sent him to confront King Ahab:

> *"As the Lord, the God of Israel, lives ... there will be neither dew nor rain in the next few years except at my word."* 1 Kings 17:1 NIV

FALSE GOD—FALSE HOPES

Stopping the rain was a judgment from God, and it touched the economy of the nation. Baal was considered to be the god of fertility and the lord of rain. Baal worship came with the promise that rain and, therefore, crop production would increase. This would help the economy. Hope for a better economy was promised if people worshiped Baal, and the entire country was seduced into believing the lie.

Once the prophet Elijah spoke, judgment came, and the rain stopped. Water is the most valuable commodity in the Middle East. If a nation is without water, animals die, and the people get sick and die. The economy of Israel was suffering because the crops had dried up. Soon there was a famine in the land, and everyone was worried. The nation was on economic alert. They were in a desperate situation.

Elijah was a man who prayed desperately for the nation of Israel, and God answered his prayers. He had power with God. For three years it did not rain, just as he said. Poverty swept through the land. King Ahab, Queen Jezebel, and their false god Baal became increasingly unpopular.

THE POWER OF ONE

How many people does it take to change a nation? Bible stories reveal that it takes one person in harmony with God to spearhead change in a nation. Noah, Abraham, Joseph, Moses, Gideon, Deborah, Daniel, Nehemiah, Ezra, David, Elijah, and Mary were all used by God to change a nation. Each of them was drawn into a desperate battle between God and Satan. Their agreement with God released his victory. They partnered with the Lord, and immeasurable blessings flowed over their generation.

When nations turn away from God, it often results in judgment and hardships intended to humble the people. Then they repent and return to the Lord. After three years of drought, Israel was ready to renounce Baal worship. Elijah was ready to lead a renewal. Judgment did not come because the nation deserved punishment. It was a demonstration of God's mercy.

JUDGMENT AND MERCY

Had the Lord not brought famine, the nation would have continued on a course of self-destruction. Baal worship would have corrupted and destroyed the people. They would have forsaken the path of civil kindness. The worship of Baal involved child sacrifice and temple prostitution. It was evil and abusive. Crime and corruption would have become rampant. In place of God's peace, demons would torment the lives of God's chosen people. Righteous living would have been replaced by immorality, which in turn would have produced spiritual and economic poverty.

Judgment was an expression of God's mercy. Elijah was God's man for that generation. He fought a desperate battle for the life of the nation. God told him to visit King Ahab again.

> "When he (Ahab) saw Elijah, he said to him, 'Is that you, you troubler of Israel?' 'I have not made trouble for Israel,' Elijah replied. 'But you and your father's family have. You have

abandoned the Lord's commands and have followed the Baals.'" 1 Kings 18:17, 18 NIV

THE DEMONS GATHER

Elijah challenged the king to gather the people of Israel for a showdown at Mount Carmel. He stood alone against 450 prophets of Baal and 400 prophets of Asherah who sat at Jezebel's table. Elijah did not know, but God had 700 of his prophets praying. Besides this, there were multitudes of his people who were ready to stand in agreement with him for spiritual renewal.

Asherah is a false god who is worshiped in many nations under different names. Besides the name Asherah or Ashterah, she is called Ishtar, Aphrodite, and Venus. She was known as the female goddess of war and fertility. She was the female consort to the demon, Baal. She was worshipped by most of the surrounding nations, including Babylon, Persia, Rome, and Greece. Worship to Asherah involved extreme lascivious practices and gross sexual perversions.

In every evil and diabolical sense of the word, Queen Jezebel, along with her Baal and Asherah gods, were demonic party gurus. With all the allurements of immediate pleasure, they seduced the masses into corruption and ruin.

JEZEBEL, BAAL AND ASHERAH TODAY

The demon spirits behind Jezebel, Baal, and Asherah function in the world today. They are enemies of every good and wholesome standard. Their schemes produce moral, spiritual, and physical death. Here is a partial list of their destructive ways.

1. They are dividers of families and breakers of homes.
2. They ruin marriages and turn parents and children against each other.

3. They hinder and stop the proper function of fertility in women, so that they cannot conceive or carry children to full term.

4. They intimidate men, so they are rendered ineffective leaders.

5. These demons do everything possible to destroy and kill any who serve the Lord.

6. Through Jezebel's witchcraft, these demons bring discouragement to men and women in the ministry, so they become disillusioned and quit.

7. Their demonic lies dilute one's faith by promoting feelings of rejection, failure, and inferiority.

8. Jezebel inspires criticism, gossip, and division among Christian workers so that friends turn against one another, and the work of the Lord is hindered.

9. She uses emotional blackmail and mind control to gain influence over people.

10. She uses witchcraft and occult practices of every sort to release her powers.

11. Her witchcraft is both overt and covert. On one hand, she casts spells and curses, calling upon her demon gods for supernatural favors.

12. On the other hand, she uses the hidden skills of witchcraft such as sexual seduction and manipulation to gain control. She promises people pleasure, then overpowers them.

RESISTING JEZEBEL

This demonic activity and these various forms of witchcraft are at work in our society undermining the good and wholesome purposes of God. They show up in many ways but are at work in every nation and on every possible front. The demons of Jezebel have built a stronghold in our society, largely through the entertainment media. This spirit has entered our homes through many doors, but the main ones are movies, television, and the Internet. Jezebel has been at work in every culture since the early days of Babylonia, but today she has found access into the homes and minds of people on a much broader scale through these electronic means.

Jezebel attacks homes, churches, business enterprises, public administrations, and political parties. Her goals are to undermine godly standards and remove the blessings of the Lord from these places.

Many good people are desperately fighting for the well-being of our nation. They embrace the principles of the Bible and lay hold of God through desperate prayer. They are ready to release renewal and revival upon the land. They recognize Jezebel, Baal, and Asherah and take a firm stand against them on behalf of their families and communities. By God's grace, they will win but not without many intense battles.

ELIJAH'S CHALLENGE

Elijah's challenge was clear and direct.

"Elijah went before the people and said, 'How long will you waver between two opinions? If the Lord is God, follow him; but if Baal is God, follow him.' " 1 Kings 18:21 NIV

The challenge was a test of supernatural power. Whose God would send down fire from heaven? Each group raised an altar and called on their God to send fire upon the altar to consume the animal sacrifice.

"At the time of sacrifice, the prophet Elijah stepped forward and prayed: 'O Lord, God of Abraham, Isaac and Israel, let it be known today that you are God in Israel.... Answer me, so these people will know that you, O Lord, are God, and that you are turning their hearts back again.' Then the fire of

the Lord fell and burned up the sacrifice." 1 Kings 18:36–38
NIV

Following the fire, all of the prophets of Baal were killed.
Then Elijah told King Ahab that the three years of drought would
end.

HEAVY RAIN

In faith, Elijah said he heard the sound of heavy rain (1
Kings 18:41).

It was time for God's blessings to fall upon the nation. Elijah
began to travail in desperate prayer. Seven times he knelt down
and put his face between his knees in urgent supplication.
Between each time he asked his servant to go and see if there
were any rain clouds approaching. After seven times, the servant saw a tiny cloud the size of a man's hand off in the distance. Before long, the sky grew black with clouds, the wind
rose, and a heavy rain fell on the land.

When Jezebel heard about the death of her prophets and
all that Elijah had done, she was incensed. She promised to kill
him. The mighty man of God ran for his life. He came under the
attack of demonic oppression. Disillusion and discouragement
overwhelmed him. He felt like quitting, and he hid in a cave. The
demons of Jezebel, stirred by witchcraft, were unrelenting in
their pursuit of him.

ANGELS ON ASSIGNMENT

The Bible story shows us the human side of the battle but
does not reveal the demonic war that raged in the unseen realms.
The book of Daniel, chapter ten, tells a story that reveals the
demonic battles behind the scenes. Powerful angels came when
Daniel prayed. They fought the demons. The more Daniel
prayed, the harder the angels fought. From all of scripture we can
conclude that Jezebel's threat to kill Elijah was real. Soldiers in

her army were looking for him, and demons in Satan's army were fighting behind the scene, adding diabolical weight to Jezebel's evil design.

Angels on assignment fought the demons, but the evil spirits did their worst. Elijah felt the pressure from both the natural and the spiritual realms. As he stepped forward to do God's will, he fought a battle on many fronts. He fought with people, with physical problems, and with demon spirits. Then God showed up in answer to his desperate prayers. He pressed through and won the battle. He prayed, and miracles came. Supernatural signs and wonders were released from heaven.

PRAYING FOR THE NATION

The spiritual battle will be no different for us and our nation. We will need perseverance, desperate prayers, and miracles to turn our generation back to God. Nothing less than the power of God with supernatural attestation will drive back the demons and capture the hearts of people. It will take miracles, but average people, sold out to God, can see miracles in answer to their desperate prayers. They can bring renewal and revival to the nation.

> "The prayer of a righteous man is powerful and effective. Elijah was a man just like us. He prayed earnestly that it would not rain, and it did not rain on the land for three and a half years. Again he prayed, and the heavens gave rain, and the earth produced its crops." James 5:16–18 NIV

PREPARING THE SOLDIERS

God is recruiting an army. Many soldiers are being trained as they battle the day-to-day struggles of life. God shows up, performs signs and wonders in their lives, and faith becomes a permanent fixture. They fight heavy battles on the home front in preparation for the war of nations.

These humble soldiers are like David, who defeated the lion and the bear while watching over his father's sheep at home. Through these backyard experiences, the men and women of God are being made ready to fight the giant, Goliath. Jesus is the captain of this army. He is preparing his people. He is the author and finisher of our faith. He has the master plan for each of our lives, and he will train us for the battles ahead.

WOUNDED SOLDIERS

There is a massive problem in the body of Christ today. It must be dealt with. Many Christians have become disillusioned and derailed, because they do not realize that their battle is not with people but with spiritual powers of wickedness. People hurt people, and too many Christians have received wounds from their own army.

People may have stopped your immediate goals, but they can never stop the destiny of God for your life. Only you can stop that. While a wounded soldier remains in his wounded state, demon spirits pummel him, and he cannot fulfill his destiny. Demon spirits gain a foothold in the lives of Christians through the following tactics:

1. Through unforgiveness, when people hurt them;
2. Through the guilt of personal sin;
3. Through feelings that God has rejected them, and his favor no longer rests on them;
4. Through the inability to deal with unfulfilled expectations.

All of these become vulnerable targets in the battle against Christians. Wounds that should not have stuck on people have indeed stuck on them. They have stuck on too many people for too long. If we allow God, he will give us a Teflon coat and not allow these things to stick on us. Forgiveness, repentance, humility, and faith will get us back on track. This is a monumental battle, but a fight that can be won by every soldier. It is time to rise up in the strength of the Lord once again.

FIGHTING BACK

Maybe you have been caught on the defensive, but it is time to move to the offensive. It is time to get back into the fight. God is with you for good and not for evil. He has a plan for your life, and you can have it, if you fight. Do not resist the Lord and his call on your life any longer. Humble yourself. Rise up and begin to walk in the plan of Christ once again. The power of God will come back into your life. Fulfill your God-given destiny.

Begin in the secret place of prayer. Continue seeking the Lord, asking him to use you. Then wait for his lead. He will show you the part that you are to play in his master design. He has perfect timing for what he wants to do, but he will do nothing without your agreement in prayer. He may help bring you to desperate prayer so that your life will make a powerful difference for good. It requires a listening ear and absolute obedience.

In his perfect time, God will bring revival to this nation and not to this nation alone but to the entire world. The glory of the Lord will cover the earth like the waters cover the sea. God will do it.

Let us intercede and supplicate for the lives of others so they will be rescued. Will you pray? Will you make yourself available for the work of the Holy Spirit? Let the Lord unfurl your destiny and calling so that you may accomplish his will. Fight for your own life in God, for your family, for your church, and for this nation. There is no greater honor and no greater adventure than to serve the Lord.